Praise for *The Missing*

● "I sing the praises of the Sensory Alphabet to everyone I can because it changed the way I think about and work with young children. It helps me go beyond the usual belief that simply giving children access to lots of materials equals creativity. Rather, this approach gave us the vocabulary to talk about children's creativity with the kids themselves, and once they know the 'words,' so to speak, they have so much to say!

The Missing Alphabet is so intuitive, you might ask yourself, 'Why haven't I realized this before?' But just as quickly, you'll begin to see the world and your child in a new way."

—Leah Hanson,
Manager of Early Learning Programs, Dallas Museum of Art

● "Come to your senses!

This engaging book invites you into a new world that can change your life!

The Sensory Alphabet is no longer a well-kept secret, explored by people identified as artists. It can become part of your cognitive and expressive repertoire. It's critical for learning science as well as art, for analysis as well as synthesis.

It is the past. And it is our future. And our children's future.

Reading and writing and arithmetic are great. But there is more. The global world requires this expansion; the digital world allows it.

Enjoy it. Engage it. Become part of it. And share the joy of your sensory environment with the young people around you."

—Kristina Woolsey, PhD,
Cofounder, Apple Multimedia Lab

● "The best ideas are simple, direct, and make you think they've been around forever. *The Missing Alphabet* offers one of those great ideas that will help parents (and teachers) build on the unique strengths of their children to help them become more creative, capable, and inquisitive learners. This book will change the way you look at the creative work of young people, and maybe more importantly, it will change what you do and say once you've seen it. A very clear approach that should be on every parent's reading list."

—Brent Hasty, PhD,
College of Education, The University of Texas at Austin

"Everything that's missing from the national conversation about education— What should our kids be learning? What skills do they need to live in a world where the only constant is change? How do they create a future for themselves?—is here in *The Missing Alphabet*. Not so much 'How to help Katie pass a standardized test'; more 'How to help Katie blossom.'"

—Emily Levine,
Comedian/philosopher

"Why is it that when you ask a room full of kids under five if any of them are creative, almost every hand in the room goes up—but when the same question is asked of middle schoolers, only one or two respond? Marcus and team, in *The Missing Alphabet*, detail the answer: we're not developing creative thinking like we need to be. And indeed, we didn't even have the language to do so—until now!

What was missing was the Sensory Alphabet. This simple but compelling framework gives parents and teachers the tools to help young kids explore and develop their native curiosity, and proven ways to help them grow their capacity for creative thinking. Supported by outstanding research in the fields of neuroscience, education, and learning, tested with real kids in real settings, the Sensory Alphabet gives parents and teachers an exciting and fresh way to build on nascent creativity.

If you have, work with, or even just know creative young kids, please, expose them to learning via *The Missing Alphabet*!"

—Dr. Larry Johnson,
Chief Executive Officer, The New Media Consortium

"In a time when schools may not be able to provide enough enrichment for young minds, *The Missing Alphabet* is a resource that parents can return to time and again, filled with everyday activities that can be custom-designed for every child."

—Meredith Brokaw,
Author of the *Penny Whistle* books for parents

"Having grown up with grandparents like Charles and Ray Eames, I had the chance to see them use many different tools—film, exhibits, photography, toys, and furniture—to communicate their ideas. As a parent myself now, I realize how important it is for a child to have a chance to try many, many new things and see what they are drawn to like a magnet.

Charles and Ray did not believe in the 'gifted few.' They believed that you got good at what you like to do. *The Missing Alphabet* offers important ways to expand the number of tools that children have in their toolbox as they make choices, both as individuals and as future global citizens."

—Llisa Demetrios,
Granddaughter of Charles and Ray Eames, and trustee of the Eames Foundation

The Missing Alphabet

The Missing Alphabet

A Parents' Guide to Developing
Creative Thinking in Kids

Susan Marcus • Susie Monday • Cynthia Herbert, PhD
FOUNDERS OF THE NEW WORLD KIDS® PROGRAM

GREENLEAF
BOOK GROUP PRESS

Published by Greenleaf Book Group Press
Austin, Texas
www.gbgpress.com

Distributed by Greenleaf Book Group LLC

For ordering information or special discounts for bulk purchases, please contact Greenleaf Book Group LLC at PO Box 91869, Austin, TX 78709, 512.891.6100.

Design and composition by Greenleaf Book Group LLC
Cover design by Greenleaf Book Group LLC

Publisher's Cataloging-In-Publication Data
(Prepared by The Donohue Group, Inc.)

Marcus, Susan, 1946-
   The missing alphabet : a parents' guide to developing creative thinking in kids / Susan Marcus, Susie Monday, [and] Cynthia Herbert. -- 2nd ed.

   p. : ill. ; cm.

   1st ed. published as: New world kids : the parents' guide to creative thinking. New York, N.Y. : Foundry Media, 2009.
   Includes bibliographical references.
   ISBN: 978-1-60832-378-4

   1. Creative thinking in children. 2. Perceptual learning. 3. Creative activities and seat work. 4. Child rearing. I. Monday, Susie. II. Herbert, Cynthia. III. Marcus, Susan, 1946- New world kids. 1st ed. IV. Title.

LB1062 .M27 2012
370.118   2012939254

Part of the Tree Neutral® program, which offsets the number of trees consumed in the production and printing of this book by taking proactive steps, such as planting trees in direct proportion to the number of trees used: www.treeneutral.com

TreeNeutral®

Printed in Singapore

12 13 14 15 16 17   10 9 8 7 6 5 4 3 2 1

Second Edition

Contents

Introduction

"Nothing's stable in the world. Uproar's your only music."
—*Keats*

"There are no passengers on spaceship earth—only crew."
—*Buckminster Fuller*

Now that we're into the second decade of the twenty-first century here on spaceship earth, this is the big picture. Change is constant and seismic on all fronts—from the weather to the economy, from food supplies to cyber attacks, from institutional meltdowns to global shifts in policies, politics, and power. On the other hand, new kinds of collaborations are leading to thrilling discoveries and inventions in many fields. It seems there is much to look forward to.

Still, assailed on all sides by such deep and relentless change, parents are rightly worried about how their children will cope with the uncertain future. Parents are caught between calls for action and conflicting messages of what to do, between hopeful new models and discouraging entrenched realities. To be sure, it's a curious time on planet earth right now.

What we do know is that this scale of change, largely driven by technology, is unprecedented in human history. And it is the change itself, this reordering, this inventing of the new world that will occupy our children's future. We are entering a time that calls for dedicated innovation across the board. This call will echo through all fields; in fact, it has already started. The child's counterpart to innovation is creative thinking, and creativity is our children's next essential literacy.

The subject of creativity, unfortunately, comes embedded with many out-of-date notions. It is often linked exclusively to the arts, or their first cousin, crafts—and then marginalized in favor of science and math, not seen as worthy enough to take up children's time in school. Ironically, while creativity is seen as a silver bullet to many future challenges, children's creative thinking skills are largely undervalued.

In the last decade, creativity has become the darling of the business world as it wrestles with the realities of the ever-changing waves of technology. Adult education has seen a surge of courses in various forms of creative thinking, and a best-selling collection of books has emerged as business leaders recognize the power of creative thinking to enable people to effect needed change and innovation.

Many parents, who are also business people, notice and worry over the disconnect between their business world and their child's school culture, which is most often still linear, abstract, and expository. This book is written to connect the dots between the innovation we need for the future and the creative thinking and working skills that we can give our kids now.

When the goal is to create a literacy in creativity, there is much that can be learned and taught. What was once a mysterious territory that belonged to artists or those who were lucky to have been born "talented," has given way to a great deal of exploration and excavation in the past few decades. Now is the time, we believe, to make the case for creativity as part of basic education for all children. To this end, we will report on some of the persuasive findings that have been brought to light in recent years in the fields of cognition, metacognition, psychology, and neuroscience. This converging evidence supports the power of creative thinking to equip children to "get in the game" of making the future

Will the institution of education deliver the next literacy? Will it be added to the traditional three Rs as a new basic for the new times? We don't know. Most of the conversation about education at this point still focuses on the "how" part of school—the mechanics of *how* we move students through the system, *how* we hire, fire, and pay teachers, *how* we test kids. Missing is the "what" part of education—*what* thinking skills and content will best equip our children to be twenty-first-century creators and inventors. Although there are some hopeful initiatives such as the Partnership for 21st Century Skills and programmatic models like Project-Based Learning and Challenge-Based Learning, widespread acceptance of creativity as a mainstream goal could be precious decades away. This is a deeply frustrating fact of life for parents whose own child's most potent learning years are quickly slipping away. These skills may well be up to parents to teach.

Creative potential is our human heritage. Every child begins life with a natural curiosity, an innate desire to learn, and an infinite potential for creative thinking and action. The ability to analyze and solve problems, to imagine and create, to explore new viewpoints and to operate in new modes of thinking and behaving is basic to us all. We all have this creative potential.

In addition, each of us has a unique set of creative strengths, with a very personal way of thinking and working that remains consistent over time and across media. This individual potential can flower most fully when it is operating with the resources that best fit each unique imagination. We believe that the greatest contributions and the deepest personal satisfaction will spring from the exercise of this creative potential.

This book is designed to help parents put their children on a path to real creative literacy—in the context of everyday life—with fun and play at the heart of the action. It is a handbook on creative thinking, a kind of "Creativity 101" for parents who want their children to be able to cope and thrive in the kaleidoscopic landscape of change we live in.

The following describes the basic organization of this book.

Part 1 begins by addressing the "what" and the "why" of creative thinking—calling attention to the part of the national conversation about education that isn't often being heard: the creative thinking skills for our children that common sense tells us we need to focus on now. What this means is we begin with our goals in mind: We want our children to be able to act creatively, to see each experience as an opportunity for invention, to be skilled at giving form to their ideas, and to have many options for communicating their ideas to other people. When our children grapple with problems, we want to see them generate not one but dozens of possible solutions. We want them to have the abilities, experience, and confidence to work from their unique constellation of strengths. We want them to know the deep satisfaction of giving their best gifts to the world. What better mental tools could we want for our kids—and for our collective future?

In part 2 we will dive into the two key concepts that make up our approach to basic creative literacy. First, we introduce the Sensory Alphabet, the building blocks for the thinking skills associated with visual, aural, and kinetic ways of learning and knowing. This "alphabet," now largely missing from our cultural awareness, is just as fundamental as the ABCs and numbers—and just as powerful. It is another symbol system you will want your children to know for expressing their ideas, innovating, creating, understanding the world around them, and even understanding themselves as thinkers and learners. The Sensory Alphabet is the foundation for creative literacy.

The second key concept is "individual creative potential." Children will need to know early on "what they are good at" and where their natural fluencies are. Brain research and studies of multiple intelligences support the idea that we all think and learn differently and that we think and learn best when we take our brain's most natural path. It is important to bring this knowing front and center now, because soon problem solving and creative work will happen most often in teams. The complex and systemic problems of the adult world need a collaborative approach. This way of thinking and working will require individuals to know what they "bring to the table," what areas they are particularly creative with, and what they can do best. This is no longer an issue that can be put off until after schooling. A child's unique brand of imagination is often correctly intuited by parents, and they are in the best position to identify these qualities early on and to provide media, materials, and experiences to feed their child's creative potential. We'll show you how.

In part 3, we'll show you "how" to put these concepts to work in the context of everyday life. Loaded with practical advice and enriching activities, this section of the book will comprise a resource that you will want to return to again and again as you plan your child's everyday experiences.

This part of the book is developed in four sections. In the first we explore the creative process—a way of thinking and a method of working long known by artists and scientists, choreographers and chefs, coaches and poets, just to name a few. And we will use this process as a guide for ways of interacting with children and structuring *open-ended activities* that will feed young imaginations and bring out unique creative responses.

In the second section we revisit the Sensory Alphabet, presenting a field guide for exploring each of its nine elements—line, rhythm, space, movement, texture, color, shape, light, and sound—in its various natural habitats in the everyday world. The zoo, museum, and even just the backyard make fertile hunting grounds and ensure that your child playfully and thoughtfully encounters this enriching alphabet.

The next section will help you identify your child's unique brand of creativity from several different vantage points. Using the Sensory Alphabet as a lens to review several case studies documented here, you will see how an individual child's strengths shine. Ideas for making observations, asking questions, and taking inventories give you resources to begin to characterize your child's distinct set of creative strengths.

The final section is about putting it all together—how to manage for creativity in the ongoing context of everyday life. Here we take the 30,000-foot view and reflect on the elements we have available to support a child's creative growth in the midst of the bustle of the everyday. These are resources we all share: time, materials, people, spaces, and interactions.

This book is designed to inform and engage parents. After all, parents are a child's first teachers. Parents teach language, including the traditional alphabet and numbers—how to be a friend, how to approach problems, what's important and what's not, the manners, mores, and other rules about how our culture works—the list goes on and on. Parents create (although not always consciously) the blueprint of values, habits, and attitudes their children live by. Children get their first indelible impressions of themselves through their parents' eyes. And so, as parents, we must recognize that it's time to enlarge our own sense of what is important now, what is to be valued and practiced, and what should be carried forward by the next generation.

It is the authors' aim as parents (and now grandparents), educators, and researchers to share the fruits of our experience with the next generation of parents. This book has grown out of decades of applied research with children, examining creativity, media, cognition, and individuality. Our work began at the Learning About Learning Educational Foundation, a future-oriented research and development institution in Texas.

Over the years, as colleagues, we worked with children, parents, teachers, schools, and educators of all kinds; created programs and materials for local, national, and global markets; and ran an influential laboratory school. We continue to work in educational settings, with schools, with after-school programs, and in museum education.

In all our years of working together, our inquiries have been based on the assumption that each child, each individual person, has abundant, powerful, and unique resources—that all of us have infinite creative potential—and that we are all mutually dependent on one another's creativity and productivity.

These beliefs and concerns have not changed—and we don't expect they will.

Susan Marcus

Susie Monday

Cynthia Herbert

Part 1

The "WHAT" and the "WHY" of Creative Thinking

"The new conditions demand a new way of thinking.
The new thinking demands new forms of expression.
The new expression generates new conditions."
—*Bruce Mau*

There's a big disconnect between how our kids need to be equipped to deal with the future and how we're preparing them now. The standards we use now were developed a century and a half ago to cope with the rise of the Industrial Revolution. It's where children learned the basic literacies of our culture related to words and numbers. The standards were fitting for that era, just what was needed then to give young people the basic skills of reading, writing, and arithmetic they would need to enter the workplace. It was also a time when the whole idea of public school was new and its institutional design reflected the "new" factory models of the time. Children were seen as empty cups to be filled with knowledge.

But, unfortunately, this approach is still the standard today, in both form and content. For the most part, we still use that same factory model in the educational system today—moving children along lock-step, all the same, like the proverbial cups to get filled up with knowledge. Our focus is still set on filling those "cups" with the same three Rs and an ever-growing accumulation of facts. Our standardized tests reflect this.

The thinking skills that are taught and applied generally fall under the umbrella of what are now called "critical thinking skills," associated with analyzing and weighing information. These skills and literacies are very important to learn, but they are no longer enough. The institution of education hasn't yet caught up with what children need to learn now to prepare them for the future where change is the only constant. It is one of the very few things that we can project about the future with some certainty. The problems that will need to be solved will undoubtedly be big, complicated, and systemic. They will clearly need solutions that call on diverse creative ideas. These are complex issues, not faced ever before on the planet. They will require systems thinking and collaboration. They will be approached by teams of diverse individuals, each bringing their individual strengths, creativity, know-how, and experience to the table—along with an agile mind that can jump the fences between categories and fields of study, over old and now bankrupt templates. We believe the most important education we can give children for the workplace of tomorrow is an understanding of, and confidence in, their individual creative potentials. This is the way we see it.

Kids today naturally gravitate into the daily world of sounds, layered images, and simultaneous events. This sensory world is up close, technological, connected, visually rich, emotional, and immediate. It's about friends, fun, computers, games, movies, stories, animals, cell phones, TV, wonders, worries, playing, communicating, family, music, and sports. It's where pop culture lives. It's also where the senses and the imagination live—*and it's where creative thinking begins.*

What we teach children has always been a blend of what parents think is important and what our culture deems necessary. We're now at a time when the institution of education has been doing "business as usual" in the face of the enormous changes that have taken place in the recent years of the digital revolution. This whole new cultural landscape is literally reshaping basic communication. Children need "new basics" in learning, a revised skill set that responds to these changes.

We believe that parents can lead the way. Now is the time for parents to take back their side of the equation by teaching relevant "new literacies" at home, in the context of the everyday—first and foremost, for their own children, and also by asking unequivocally for it to happen in educational settings now—at school, in after school programs, and in other learning environments like museum summer camps and children's museums. (This book will give you what you need to know.)

Our culture is ready for a change. Wrenching documentary films like *Waiting for "Superman"* and white papers like the Gates Foundation study "The Silent Epidemic" (2006) regarding high dropout rates give ample and dramatic indications of the need for a kind of education that responds to the basic needs for new understandings, greater personal meaning and significance, and more and deeper connections with the world we live in—a dramatic world of contrasting

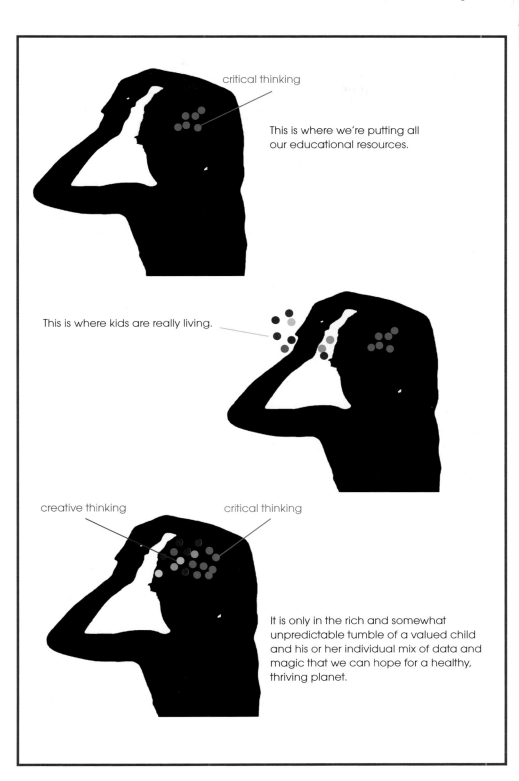

critical thinking

This is where we're putting all our educational resources.

This is where kids are really living.

creative thinking

critical thinking

It is only in the rich and somewhat unpredictable tumble of a valued child and his or her individual mix of data and magic that we can hope for a healthy, thriving planet.

landscapes, both natural and digital, beckoning with both huge problems to solve, and, at the same time, breathtaking opportunities.

But first a quick review. How did we get here?

Thinking Historically

It's useful to take a big step back and remember one important thing: Educating the next generation has always been done by parents who want the best for their children. Parents in every epoch have decided what skills children needed to grow up and be successful. These choices have changed and morphed over generations, responding to the cultural differences and needs of the time. Although our current system has roots in the Industrial Age, there were other models of learning that preceded it.

In many cultures, to be literate—to have the abilities to interpret, manipulate, communicate, and create with symbols—is not necessarily attached to the symbols of words and numbers as it is in our culture. Today over 80 percent of the people on the planet can actually read and write, but all have developed abilities to use other kinds of symbols to communicate their ideas.

Deep in the past, other literacies held sway. The animal drawings on the cave walls made 15,000 years ago speak volumes about the people's reverence and awe for the animals they saw and hunted. A crucial *visual literacy* was then embedded in how they tracked game, read the clouds, studied the patterns in the stars, and learned from the mathematical elegance of the plants and the seasons. This literacy was expressed in their exquisite drawings, in the patterns we see in baskets, weavings, and pottery, and in the ways they lived in accord with nature.

Likewise, the oral traditions of the indigenous world were grounded in the stories told around the fire that held the mythological and metaphorical symbols that imparted the meanings and values that children needed to grow up successfully. The listening, remembering, telling, and retelling of those important stories embodied a kind of *aural literacy* we can only imagine. It is lost to most of us now, not because the capacity isn't there, but because it is no longer valued.

Along the way, the invention of the various alphabets and writing forms gave people new means of symbolizing and recording information, events, stories, and ideas. These records and messages could then be saved and transported over distances. Numbers symbolized and streamlined calculations and transactions. Over time, the symbol systems we use today—the alphabet and numbers—came to be chosen as the ones to teach and pass on.

By the nineteenth century, when public school was invented, it was clear that the thinking skills that had turned these symbol systems into powerful literacies were the most valued, and so they were selected as the skills the children should acquire to ensure success as adults in their commerce with the world. The three Rs were born. In the context of education, visual and aural knowing (i.e., *sensory literacy*) was neglected. These choices are still with us today. *Literacy* (verbal skills) and *numerancy* (number skills) continue to be the basis of our schooling.

The Digital Tsunami

Although our approach to schooling has remained the same over the past century, diverse forces have appeared that have dramatically changed the landscape of our culture and how we interact with it. The digital media of today had roots in older technologies. Film—embodying sound, motion, image, and storytelling—is known to powerfully influence the culture; likewise, television. More sophisticated color printing technologies, combined with the economic success of the advertising industries, have spawned a growing deluge of images on almost every surface and screen.

When digital media first came on the scene, it was mostly geared to computation. But as the computing power continued to rise, the size and cost of computers continued to shrink. The larger byte budget needed for imaging could be accommodated, and the smaller footprints of the machines made them fitting for home use. In time, they were adopted by our culture, a little at first, a lot as the interfaces became simpler and more "friendly"—more human. Computers, now fast and powerful tools for working with words, numbers, images, video, and sound, have been universally adopted by the population for an ever-growing cascade of possibilities. Computers have become indispensable partners at work and at home.

Cell phones, tiny computers themselves, have also had global adoption. Almost every mobile device now contains still and video cameras and the means to send and receive images, as well as video, audio, text, and numerical data. GPS (Global Positioning Systems), with the ability to locate the precise position of a mobile device via satellite, unfolds the spatial dimension for mapping, locating friends, and referencing places—another myriad of possibilities. Anyone with a cell phone holds in their hand the possibility of being a communicator, a photographer, a videographer, a writer, a geographer, a publisher, a mathematician, and countless other choices.

The newest mass-market digital media is the tablet, now being massively adopted. When paired with "the cloud," which can put much of the functionality of computing onto the Internet, all this can be had at a very modest price. The explosion of the "app" world extends the possibilities even further. And the near ubiquity of wireless environments makes it all even more immediate.

The planet is going digital. The pervasive Internet, providing global interconnectivity, has launched a universal rethinking of our relationship to how we get and give information and ideas across all platforms—business, mass media, education, politics, the arts, our sense of community—everything.

When you look at it from our 30,000-foot perspective, the past few decades of change seem cataclysmic, and yet technology savants say we're still at the beginning of this digital tsunami. In relationship to the discussion of "new literacies," several important factors in our brief digital survey stand out:

1. Images and sound, in all their forms, are just as important (if not more so) than words and numbers in their power to capture attention, communicate information and ideas, and change behavior.
2. Using, creating, and sharing images, words, video, and sounds (both talk and music) via digital media is now mainstream among young people. They've adopted the media and the mindset and are collectively aware that this is *the future*. This genie is way out of the bottle.
3. It's a global phenomenon.

What this means for today's children is that they are truly living in a new world. We've come a long way from the few short decades ago when computers were the provenance of science, industries, and governments—used exclusively for computational purposes. And we've also traveled a long way from the time when the desktop computer made its way into the home and taught us all to type on keyboards and play Pacman.

As the Internet has become available to all and introduced digital communication, e-mail eclipsed "snail mail," and now mobiles offer the ubiquitous texting. All of this is to say digital technology is now a digital *landscape,* and we are living in "digital soup." The new world our children are living in is animated as much by technology as the Industrial Age was by machines.

And while the Industrial Age drove our literacy choices for schooling, the sweeping and ongoing changes of our Digital Age are driving our need for innovation. And the need for *innovation education* is beginning to be felt.

The Business of Business Is Now Innovation

Today's business world has been coping with the climate of drastic change for decades, driven by the rolling waves of new technologies, the new discoveries, and then the shifting perspectives that inevitably follow. For business, innovation is a matter of survival. The best thinking of business leaders has shown them that teaching *creative thinking skills* will provide the most valuable tools for their employees. Dozens of "creativity colleges" now help adults in the business sector master these qualities of thinking.

Creativity has also been found to be key not only to an effective workforce but also to effective leadership. Recently, IBM asked 1,500 corporate heads and public sector leaders from sixty nations and thirty-three industries what they felt was now the most important leadership quality for success in business today. At the top of the list was creativity. Even in the context of appalling economic conditions, CEOs found creativity more valuable than *management discipline, existing best practices, rigor,* or *operations* (Carr, 2010).

Daniel Pink's groundbreaking 2005 book, *A Whole New Mind: Why Right-Brainers Will Rule the Future*, also spotlights innovation by presenting the coming new era as the "Conceptual Age," predicting that it will be characterized as both *high-concept* and *high-touch*. His recommendation, for those who want to survive and thrive in the future: Educate the right-brain capacities of *"inventiveness, empathy, joyfulness,* and *meaning"* that have been largely ignored in favor of our lopsided focus on the left-brain abilities of critical thinking, reasoning, and judging.

Another striking recommendation for inventiveness, meaning, and downright fun is from Jane McGonigal, director of game research and development at the Institute for the Future at Stanford, who tells us to rethink our beliefs about what video games have to offer. The digital game industry is a behemoth, where we currently and collectively spend over three billion hours a week, despite the current general consensus that games are just *games,* an empty pastime. In contrast to this assumption, McGonigal makes an eloquent case that when we (and that includes many, many young people) are in a game world, we are motivated to do something that matters, inspired to collaborate and cooperate, likely to help at a moment's notice, driven to stick with a problem as long as it takes, and feel empowered after failure to get up and try again. In games, she suggests, we are the best version of ourselves (TED talk, 2010).

Not only that, but in the game world we can have the heightened experience called *fiero*. The Italian word for "pride," it's what happens when we triumph over adversity. We typically throw our arms over our head and yell. Neuroscientists have documented fiero as one of the most powerful neurochemical highs we can experience. And that's not surprising, since it happens in the part of the brain associated with reward and addiction. In short, games call on our creativity, invite us to challenges that test our abilities, and reward our daring. In games we have *hard fun* (*Reality Is Broken*, 2011). No wonder so many of our young people spend so much time there.

Where Innovation Begins

For business, "innovation" is often understood as bringing new methods, products, or ideas into a field or industry that has already been established. It assumes a familiarity with the information and processes that exist. It's a new step forward— it might be a baby step or a giant leap. But it's a grown-up idea.

The child's counterpart to the business world's concept of innovation is *creative thinking*. Practicing creative thinking can hone the natural tendencies for invention that we see so often in children's play into a firm foundation of thinking skills that will serve them (and us) in the future.

And it's not a matter of chance or talent or luck; creative thinking is a matter of focus and practice. Like reading, it's a skill that is learned by doing. Inborn imagination and natural creativity become fluent thinking tools when children learn to see patterns, use associative thinking, and practice creating. Also, just like reading, adults help kids along by supplying the right challenge at the right time.

Let's take our reading example a bit further. It's a skill built on the foundation of several diverse

Educational researchers have recognized the importance of creativity in the twenty-first century and put it at the top of the well-known Bloom's Taxonomy, a pyramid of thinking skills, arranged in order of complexity and importance. Creating, in this framework, is classified higher than evaluating, analyzing, applying, understanding, and remembering (Anderson et al. 2000).

elements: You have to know the squiggles that make up the alphabet. You have to remember the sounds associated with those abstract symbols. Then you have to understand how words are constructed out of the symbols, and finally the way to move your eye along the line of letters to come up with the sounds that make the words like spoken words. You build these sensibilities a little at a time. Somewhere along the way, meanings start to pop into your brain and—*presto!*—you're reading! You get better at it as you practice—that's just how it works.

Skill at creative thinking works the same way. Like reading, it's grounded in diverse elements. It's enhanced by a sensory vocabulary (elemental building blocks, like the alphabet) and through experiences with a kind of thinking not necessarily involved with words—the kinds of knowing that your senses and your body are good at, like riding a bike, judging the relative weights of two objects, or seeing your favorite color. Often some kind of media comes next—like pencils or cameras or drums—as a way for ideas to get from inside your head to outside your head and into the world—to take form. Creative thinking (often in the presence of a problem to solve) consciously rubs these diverse elements together and—*presto!*—ideas, meanings, solutions, or maybe inventions start to pop into your brain.

Creative thinking is a generative process. It honors intuition but doesn't leave out analysis. It uses data but also looks for larger patterns. It is flexible and fluent. It is the kind of thinking that is the foundation for innovation in all fields, from physics to engineering, from genetics to technology. It is a most sought-after quality in the current business environment. And yet, it's not often taught in our schools.

Something about Education

Many parents, also part of the business community, are aware of the deep dichotomy between their fast-changing work environment and their children's school culture. In the educational world, time has stood still. Here, most often, the thinking that is rewarded is still linear, abstract, and expository. The fiero that is experienced in the gaming world is not a word you would often associate with schools today.

Sir Ken Robinson is an internationally known speaker and writer on creativity. He expertly frames the issues facing business and education in the new global economies. In article entitled "Transform Education? Yes, We Must" (Huffington Post, January 11, 2009), he makes the stakes clear:

> *To face the future, America needs to celebrate and develop the diverse talents*
> *of all its people . . . It needs to cultivate creativity and innovation, systemati-*
> *cally and with confidence . . . in rebuilding its post-industrial communities . . .*
> *Basic . . . is a different view of human talent and ability, and of the real condi-*
> *tions in which people flourish.*

There are promising initiatives on the horizon. The Partnership for 21st Century Skills, a nonprofit coalition sponsored by business, education, and community has developed a widely accepted framework of needed skills for the twenty-first-century workplace. These skills include creativity and innovation, visual literacy, problem solving, and cross-disciplinary thinking.

New programmatic models like Project-Based Learning and Challenge-Based Learning demonstrate that needed skills can be more easily picked up almost as a by-product of working on an absorbing challenge. Children in these programs bring their natural creative thinking to bear on real problems such as water quality or the energy needs of a specific location. They work in teams, investigate in different fields of study, research what's new, and try out new viewpoints and possibilities. Students then create real-world solutions, make models of their ideas, and learn to present them. And they undoubtedly have a good chance at fiero.

Unfortunately, this approach doesn't represent the curricula experienced by the vast majority of kids in America. Will our schools change fast enough for the children of the concerned parents who are reading this book? Probably not. In the race for innovation, we are leaving the children behind.

This Is Where Parents Come In

Every parent is aware of how quickly childhood slips by. Museum, after-school, and summer programs are sometimes geared to supplying experiences that meet these twenty-first-century needs, but a comprehensive child-based approach is usually not possible within the context of these brief encounters. In all likelihood, for the foreseeable future, it will be up to parents to teach their children creative thinking skills.

If the thought of this seems daunting, remember: Parents are a child's first teachers. Parents teach language and communication. Parents teach every child their mother tongue, the alphabet, and numbers. (Can't you sing the "alphabet song" in your head right now? Or remember the bright plastic numbers clinging to the refrigerator door?)

The good news is that kids live and breathe this creative thinking already. It's as basic as its more trusted counterpart, critical thinking. Humans come by it naturally; it's part of our human nature. We just don't honor it or educate it. In fact, research tells us this kind of thinking is almost squeezed out of our kids by the time they reach fourth grade. This is where parents can play a crucial role.

We all want to see our kids grow up happy and successful. But now the game is changing. Success may well rely on rethinking what is needed now and adding creative thinking to the list of skills that is practiced and applauded. Schools are focused elsewhere. It's up to parents to fill this gap. If parents don't give kids a strong foundation in creative thinking, they probably won't get it. If parents don't *value* creativity, kids won't either. It's that simple.

It's time to open this conversation about kids and future-oriented skills with parents. In fact, it's past time. The world has changed a great deal since the institution of public school was designed, verbal and numerical literacies were selected as the most important to be taught, and the basic curriculum of the three Rs was set. As parents, it's time to step outside of the academic box we've built for our culture in the last centuries. As parents, we must reconsider what we want and need to give our children to carry forward.

We believe it's time to rethink "the basics"—to incorporate, teach, and value the kinds of skills that are on the creative thinking side of the spectrum, as well as the critical thinking side. That's a challenge for our culture, which often views creativity with suspicion. Although we admire shining examples of creative achievement, we tend to believe it's a mysterious process—or even more magical, a matter of that elusive thing called *talent*. And besides, it's hard to measure.

But alone, the standard three Rs won't take us where we need to go. The facts, figures, and unconnected blueprints of subjects that currently make up the typical school curriculum create only a still image in a motion-picture world that is instead liquid and changing.

Along with traditional critical thinking skills, it's now essential to add: building observation skills; playing with many media; creating and re-creating; making connections; messing up; approaching a subject sideways; and solving a problem from the inside out. This approach is about learning a sensory vocabulary, perceiving larger patterns, and jumping mental fences. It's also about allowing intuition, putting your hands in and applying your unique fingerprints—in other words, the goal is to develop the kinds of thinking that are fluent enough to come up with the innovations the future will demand.

Digital Parents

Despite our continued dependence on verbal literacy, much of the information that surrounds us is nonverbal. And today's youth are far ahead of us in adopting the use of sound and images. They are "out there," living passionately in the world saturated with pictures, communication, music, and video. This is the world that their senses report to be valid and important. And it is very often delivered on the screens of digital media.

Most kids are completely at home with technology in a way that their parents, who did not grow up with such pervasive technology, may not be. As a result, adults—teachers and parents alike—often assume that the versatility kids show in *manipulating* digital technology also means that they are equally versatile in *thinking* with technology. But this is not necessarily the case. The world of apps often delivers the barest forms of interactivity. The repetition of many games and the fill-in-the-blank quality of much educational software calls on very low levels of thinking and has the effect of keeping the user in the role of consumer rather than that of creator.

Computers are the most powerful tools we have had in all of human history. Unlike any generation before, children can access all human knowledge. With these machines, they can explore, create, compose, invent, and communicate. The whole world is literally at their fingertips. Much of this knowledge is delivered onscreen in visual form. Video arguably captures and communicates more and different information than words in print. Color, movement, sound, and storytelling has the capacity to engage emotion and produce a more complex, and for many, a more memorable effect. It is closer to a *felt experience,* one that is sensory.

The need to author in nonverbal formats will become more and more important in the future. (For instance: How do you express a feeling with color when you need to make a multimedia school report? How can you use shape to define "amounts" in an infographic? How can you edit a video to create a rapid and exciting pace?) This content—all the images, icons, sounds, and video—enters our brains through our senses, all simultaneously and nonlinearly. Paradoxically, educating the senses is what provides the richest foundation for working creatively with digital media.

We adults have a very significant role to play in fostering children's sensory development, based on our own experiences working with traditional media. But often, we are hesitant to embrace these new tools, assuming we have nothing to add. It is useful to remember that it is the content that pours out of the digital media that we are concerned with, not the digital media itself. The need to be versatile, creative thinkers with appreciation and mastery of sensory data is far reaching. A much-needed understanding of other people, other cultures, even our planet derives from being able to decode or "read" sensory perceptions. Our effectiveness as a country in collaborating, problem solving, and inventing in "the global village" will be affected by our children's level of expertise with sensory-based information that is *beyond words.*

An emphasis on sensory understandings is not currently a part of the culture of education, but we believe that it is a vital part of what kids need now, and the foundation of building a literacy of creativity. As the designer and futurist, Bruce Mau, put it succinctly: *"Creativity is not device-dependent."*

Creativity: The Bigger Picture

Creativity is basic. We're all born creative. It's our inheritance as humans, as fundamental as eating, sleeping, and breathing. We all have the capacity to analyze and solve problems, to explore new perspectives, to operate in new modes of thinking and behaving, to imagine and invent. Our understanding of creativity encompasses the notion of putting the imagination to work, of bringing ideas into the world, and making them tangible. Generation after generation of humans has inherently understood this. Now science can add to that understanding.

The next four sections approach different aspects of creativity. Experts studying the mind and brain have added a great deal of information that highlights the importance of creativity to thinking and learning. Here are some of their key findings.

THINKING AND LEARNING ARE CREATIVE PROCESSES

Thinking and learning in themselves are acts of creation. For example, consider how we see, hear, and otherwise sense the world around us. We don't just see what is there—we add meaning to what we see. We go beyond the information given. For a simple example, look at the following array of dots. We do not merely see a jumble of dots; in our mind's eye, we create four vertical lines. The lines are not actually there, but the way our brains are designed, we literally "connect the dots."

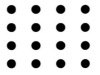

We see, to some degree, what we expect to see and remember from past experiences and what we want to see. Our perceptions are colored by (and created from) our natural strengths, our preferences, and our prejudices. Because of this, eyewitness testimonies are notoriously faulty. People don't just remember *better* or *worse* than others, they remember—and re-create—experiences *differently* (Neisser, 1999).

Likewise, learners construct (create) their own knowledge. Learning is not a matter of squeezing information into an empty head. Children must literally create (and re-create) what they learn (Bransford et al, 2000). Consider a child's understanding of "dog." The idea of "dog-ness" is created from many real-life experiences, as well as from lots of stories both heard and read by the child. As that idea develops, it is mixed with all the child's feelings and opinions about dogs. The concept grows as the child grows, and it is far richer than a dictionary definition. Most children can recognize dogs even if they don't have four legs and cannot bark. Your child's notion of "dog-ness" is her unique creation, and that will never be exactly the same as your own or anyone else's.

> Current brain research and cognitive psychology tell us that human beings can learn only very low-level tasks and ideas through drill and rote memorization. For learning to be faster, longer lasting, and of a higher order, each of us must "construct" our own personally meaningful definitions. Although we will all have common notions, the depth and variety of our experiences will determine the depth and dimensionality of our understanding (Herbert, 2009).

Concepts that are more abstract, such as "number" or "justice" are created in the same way. People may create similar concepts, but they are, in fact, distinctly and inherently individual. For example, if you have a natural talent or history of success in mathematics, the concept of "number" you create may define numerals as interesting symbols that make intriguing patterns. If, on the other hand, your experiences with math were largely negative, you may still know what a number is, but the concept you create will be more limited and less engaging. The same is true for "justice": A victim will create a much different concept for justice than will a criminal (Herbert, 2009).

Even long-term memories are created. Instead of files containing unchanging data or photo albums of unchanging pictures, our minds subtly and unconsciously alter and "Photoshop" the past to reflect a changing sense of one's self and the world (Sousa, 2006).

CREATIVITY IS INESCAPABLY ENTWINED WITH INDIVIDUALITY

Each one of us has a brain that is creating constantly and uniquely. And each one of us has a diverse array of strengths as singular and enduring as a fingerprint. This personal interior architecture plays out in countless individual ways of thinking and working that appear to be natural and inborn. In adults, we see this every day. It's clear that a choreographer's creativity with *movement* is not the same as an architect's creativity with *space*. A novelist's imagination with the *linear* form of storytelling is in stark contrast with a landscape designer's imagination with *texture*. As adults, we prize these highly individual brands of creativity. When someone's natural creativity is something that our culture appreciates, we call that person "talented."

But, for most of us, it's not until we're out of school as young adults that individuality becomes an important factor in our thinking. Only then do we begin to try to figure out what we're good at, where our talents lie. Better late than never, we start on the mission to *find ourselves*. Armed with little information about this from school experience, we might try the pinball approach, bouncing from one job to the next, looking for that *good fit*. This can be a disheartening approach. But it doesn't have to be this way.

We know, by heart and by experience, that when we are operating in our own particular way, we are tapped into our special imagination—we have a fountain of ideas, a flood of energy, and we do our best and most creative work. When we are going with the grain, we are fluent, focused, and engaged. When we apply those qualities to work that has personal meaning, we experience fiero!

The opposite also happens. When we are going against the grain, denying our unique style of thinking and working, we are unable to find and use that connection to our imagination. We have less energy and fewer ideas; we feel that our work is diminished and not our personal best. If this continues for a long time, we can even experience depression and burnout. If fiero and burnout represent opposite ends of a wide-ranging creativity spectrum, we would all agree that we prefer to be operating more toward the fiero end of that spectrum, enjoying work/play and hard fun, doing what we're good at—giving the best of ourselves.

Mihaly Csikszentmihalyi, creativity expert, calls it "flow," and said this: "Creativity is a central source of meaning in our lives... (and) when we're creative, we feel we are living more fully than during the rest of life." (Csikszentmihalyi, 1990)

Very young children experience plenty of fiero. Their work/play is clearly important to them, and they are also aware that it's important to their parents as well. They are learning how to move, walk, talk, listen, learn, decipher their environment, and communicate their needs and desires— in short, they are learning how to be "players" in their world—each in his or her own particular way. Research tells us that, for most people, the height of creativity occurs before seven years of age, before traditional education begins to label and classify us.

Before going to school, young minds have spent years growing at an astonishing pace, expanding their creative powers, understanding more and more about their world. But when children enter the world of school, they encounter demands for a linear, expository way of learning that is foreign and disconnected from their own strengths and their own experience thus far. In this world, children are seen uniformly as Students. Individual differences in the ways that children learn are not often on the front burner. Children become part of the schools' factory model, where there is one way to learn, the three Rs are the basics, and growing skills are measured on a linear scale with numbers. We have to find ourselves after our schooling journey is over because we've lost ourselves along the way.

School learning is too often lacking in personal significance. Our current educational system rewards a certain kind of academic achievement. And its linear viewpoint, its way of measuring skills or even intelligence, is out of date. Research shows us that there is very little correlation between what we call "smart" (IQ) and success later in life. Longitudinal studies have shown that a much higher correlation for success in life comes from employing creative thinking.

Parents play a key role here. They often accurately intuit their child's particular strengths. They know where his imagination is full and flowing and what her favorite work/play is. But here's the problem: This parental understanding is often at odds with what school tells us is important. Over the years we've let those test scores take on a vital importance and allowed our intuition to take a back seat. For many children (and their parents) test scores have come to define who is "smart" and who isn't. This perception is often erroneous, and it can have deeply affecting consequences. For young children, at this critical time of life, lasting mental blueprints are being laid down that will strongly influence the rest of each child's development on all levels. Identities can be at stake. As a country, we can no longer afford for so many kids to grow up thinking they are lacking when they are not.

As we look at how to build a literacy of creativity, it becomes clear that how we approach individuality is a central piece of the puzzle. In part 3, parents will learn ways of identifying those unique brands of creativity in their children. We believe that Einstein summed it up perfectly: *"Everyone is a genius. But if you judge a fish by its ability to climb a tree, it will spend its whole life thinking it is stupid."*

CREATIVITY IS A WAY OF THINKING AND A METHOD OF WORKING

The creative process has long been known. It starts with an impulse, a notion, a question, a need. You begin the process by using all your senses, memories, and feelings to *collect*—information, ideas, hunches, possibilities, materials. You're working with a kind of thinking that is not necessarily involved with words—the kinds of knowings that your senses and your body are good at—like balancing on one foot or judging the right texture of

Creative activity enriches the brain. According to neuroscientists, whether we invent with sounds, colors, words, or movement, creative work adds to our creative networks of ideas and enriches the brain. Neurons grow and make new connections as our children create forms of all kinds: drawings, constructions, songs, dramas, dances, machines, stories, social forms, solutions to problems, and so on (Jensen, 1999; 2001).

Because learning is so creative, experts underscore the vital need for active participation in the learning process if we hope to raise productive, innovative individuals (Bruner, 1966; Piaget, 1974; Vygotsky, 1978; Gardner, 1999).

the dough or sensing the effects of different colors. This feeds your imagination. We call it *priming*.

Next comes *play*. You begin to play with your collections. You brainstorm, make associations, notice patterns, make new relationships. You give your imagination free rein, often adding some kind of media to the mix, something that jump-starts your ideas—like pencils or numbers, a camera or a drum. This is a way for ideas that are inside your head to come out into the world, to become tangible. Playing lets you try out ideas without expectations or consequences. Mess around. Mess up. Play. Creative thinking consciously (and sometimes subconsciously) tosses these diverse elements together and—presto!—ideas start to bubble up.

Then the mind is primed to *create*. Now you select, add, choose, take away, shape, edit—you create a form for your idea. This can mean a dance, an essay, a recipe, a costume, a circuit board, a performance, a painting—you get the picture. The process is the same, no matter the final form. After that, you might polish up your creation to get it ready for a larger audience or save it for the future in your pool of possibilities.

The last (and often neglected) step is *reflection*. When we give tangible form to our ideas, we are not only designing, expressing, and communicating but also giving ourselves perspective toward ongoing experience. A form, once produced, becomes part of the texture of experience, a resource of new information. It shows us what has passed and suggests directions for the future. Reflection has an unanticipated benefit as well: As we learn to comprehend our creative process and products, we are simultaneously learning more about ourselves as unique creative beings. Reflected in our work, we begin to see our own strengths as thinkers.

Creative thinking is a generative process. It relies on the imagination but tempers it with analysis. It uses all kinds of information but also looks for larger patterns. It is flexible and fluent. Its products are legion. It is the kind of thinking that is the foundation for innovation in all fields, from physics to engineering to cooking to painting to law. It is a sought-after skill, and it is teachable—in the same way we teach the scientific method. We will explore the creative process further in Part 3.

CREATIVITY CAN BE A LITERACY

As educators seek to build the traditional literacies in children, there are two simple but profound steps involved. And parents most often teach the all-important first step. We'll use *reading* here as the example of a literacy to explain:

- Step 1—The foundation for a literacy is a "symbol system." In the case of reading, specific lines make up the alphabet. In our culture, it is the familiar *ABCs*; in other cultures, there are other symbols. Some are more pictorial in nature, like the Asian characters that reference images; others are sound specific, like musical notes (which serve the same function as an alphabet.) Still other symbol systems are lines or shapes that designate movement and direction. We often use arrows for this. Highway signs are a familiar example. Dancers and football players have their own variations on this idea to communicate movement in their fields. (More about symbol systems in Part 2.)
- Step 2—The next step is to teach the thinking skills that our culture uses in coordination with a symbol system. For reading, those thinking skills revolve around children learning to decode those symbols they've learned and to understand the meanings that are attached to the words they make. Many other skills are built on these basics, from phonetics to grammar, from composing an essay to creating a poem. We call the person who can comprehend information through written words and communicate information and ideas in writing with a certain level of expertise "verbally literate."

To develop a literacy of creativity, we also start with step 1, in this case the Sensory Alphabet—the basic building blocks for creating all forms, and that includes reading, writing, and arithmetic as well. The Sensory Alphabet is the foundation for decoding, comprehending, and communicating with images and other kinds of nonverbal information. This can mean anything from paintings to infographics. Then, in step 2, we teach and practice the creative process, which includes generating ideas and solutions and giving them form.

These two basic steps—the symbol system that is the Sensory Alphabet and the creative process of thinking and working—will take us to a basic literacy of creativity. This lays the groundwork for real creative thinking in most fields of work and study.

It is clear that in a school setting, concentrating only on academic strengths is no longer enough. Aptitudes in reading and math fail to reflect the full range of human creative capacity. When you consider the unknowns of the future, it is only common sense that the basic curriculum should include the symbol system of the senses (the Sensory Alphabet) and the diverse creative thinking skills that go with this symbol system. This can put us on a path to a real literacy of creativity. These are the perceptual, cognitive, creative, and communicative tools (tuned to individual strengths) that are needed for growing up right now in our landscape of constant change, and for leading us into the future. Creativity is a fundamental need now. It is our next essential literacy and part of the new basics. Here's the way we see it:

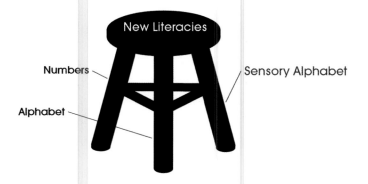

The sturdy stool of the new literacies, needed now for all children, rests on three symbol systems: the traditional alphabet, numbers, and the Sensory Alphabet. Parents, again, play a key role in making this a reality for children. And what is the realm of parents? They operate in the context of everyday life—the comings and goings, front doors and back doors, streets and sidewalks, family and friends, waking and sleeping, rituals and rhythms, sound and silence, pets and playtimes, conversations and celebrations—the beginnings, middles, and ends that make up our "everydays." It is these everydays we have to work with.

And, as parents, when we consider how to teach another symbol system and to support our own children's creative thinking, the first question that comes to mind is: How does creative thinking manifest itself on an everyday basis? What are we looking for in our children? What is the big picture?

This is what we're talking about: our goals for creative kids.

Goals for Creative Kids

- We want our children to be able to act creatively every day, to see each experience as an opportunity for inventing, to be skilled at giving form to their ideas.
- We want our children to have many options for communicating their ideas to other people, to be experienced with many media.

- When our children grapple with problems, we want them to be able generate not just one, but dozens of possible solutions.
- We want our children to have the abilities, experience, and confidence to work from their unique constellation of strengths.
- We want our children to have the profound satisfaction of giving their best gifts to the world.

We need all the children now. We need all their best, creative thinking. The world needs all their special gifts. For now, parents are the key to making this happen. What you need to know for your own child is in the next chapters.

"Our task, regarding creativity, is to help children climb their own mountains, as high as possible. No one can do more."
                    —*Loris Malaguzzi, Founder of Reggio Emilio*

Part 2

The Missing Pieces: Two Key Ingredients for a Literacy of Creativity

*"There are children playing in the street who could
solve my top problems in physics because they have
modes of sensory perception that I lost long ago."*
—J. Robert Oppenheimer

We think in more than one way—we think in all the ways we experience the world. We think in pictures, in sound, in movement. We think spatially, kinetically, and texturally. We literally think with our whole bodies! But in our culture we honor and educate the linear and abstract thinking that is most characteristic of our academic model. This is not enough to engage creative thinking. We must educate our whole selves—all the ways of knowing. This chapter begins with a vocabulary that underlies and informs all these knowings; we call it the Sensory Alphabet—the *missing alphabet.*

Another fundamental but missing piece concerns the role individuality plays in creative thinking and learning. For example, the creative architect's passion for *space* and *light* will not register on standardized tests. The creative scientist who makes a new discovery in biology may be relying more on his particular sensitivity to *movement* and the observation skills he learned in his art class. The importance of this piece—of a child's seemingly innate strengths, preferences, and interests—is now fortified by neuroscience. Individuality matters—both to your child's well-being and to our collective future. It is the second missing piece.

Parents play a key role in noticing and supporting their child's individual brand of creativity, in bringing back the "missing person."

Perhaps, most important of all, we've found that both these missing pieces are welcome news to kids, many of whom are deeply worried about *measuring up*. The idea that everyone learns differently and has special strengths opens up new horizons for them. It opens the door to a greater enjoyment and understanding of human diversity. It gives them a vision of what they might have to contribute in the future.

1. The Missing Alphabet

Let's start with the first missing piece, the set of fundamental symbols that are largely absent from our sensory vocabulary, our way of understanding and approaching the world around us—the Sensory Alphabet. This "alphabet" makes up the most basic building blocks of this multiple-ways-of-knowing approach. It is the basis of our sensory connection with the world. It has the same relationship in this approach as the traditional alphabet does to reading. It is a set of attributes elemental to our planet. It's how our senses report to our brains what is out there. It's how we can describe the qualities of anything and everything. The Sensory Alphabet is not a process or method; however, it's the place to begin.

There are nine elements in the Sensory Alphabet: *line, rhythm, space, movement, texture, color, shape, light,* and *sound*. In design parlance, these elements are the "givens." *Everything* can be described in these terms. And though they are familiar, most of us don't explore their powers or use them consciously for problem solving and creating.

Our brains work so quickly and efficiently to construct meaning around our perceptions of the world that often we don't notice the elemental qualities of our experience. We immediately and unconsciously leap right into defining, labeling, and judging. We don't see the bowl of yellow *shapes*, we see *lemons*. We don't see the green prickly *lines* on a tree, we see *pine needles*. We don't hear the *rhythm* that makes Texans want to dance, we hear the *two-step*.

And so, from babyhood on, we are off on our lifelong journey of naming, labeling, and pigeonholing the world around us. It's the perceptual shorthand we need and use so that we don't have to focus on every little thing. But it is also the template for thinking *inside the box*. And when our goal is building a literacy of creativity, we must return to a more elemental approach.

The Sensory Alphabet can be thought of as a *symbol system*—a set of symbols that we can use to communicate information and ideas. The two other symbol systems that immediately spring to mind are the traditional alphabet (the *ABCs*) and numbers. But there are many more. Next, we will take a small detour to remind ourselves of some of the symbol systems we use in this culture:

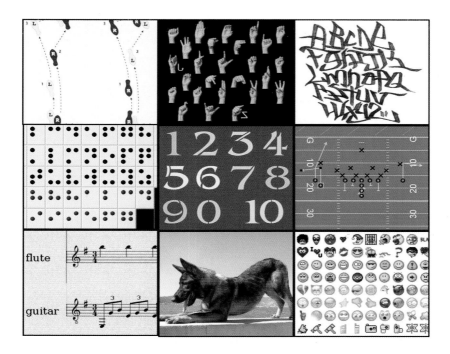

You are probably familiar with these symbol systems that we use on a daily basis, although some you may know more intimately than others. Clockwise from the upper left, they are as follows:

1. Notations for a dance—in this case, the tango
2. Gestures that comprise American Sign Language
3. Our alphabet
4. A description of football plays
5. "Emoticons"—to communicate emotions via a keyboard
6. "Dog speak"—one of many gestures—this one invites play
7. Musical notation, signifying specific sounds and pacing
8. Braille, a way of expressing the alphabet through touch
9. Numbers, symbolizing amounts

The two symbol systems all our schools teach now are the *traditional alphabet* and *numbers*. The following chart reminds you how these systems work:

Symbol System	Media	Forms
TRADITIONAL ALPHABET	spoken words (language)	oratory, songs, conversations, etc.
	written words	contracts, books, texting, grocery lists, reports, etc.
NUMBERS	algebra, arithmetic, geometry, etc.	cosmology, accounting, scorekeeping, timekeeping, bank statements, physics, etc.
SENSORY ALPHABET	cameras, paint, fabric, computers, pencils, paper, "stuff"	gardening, carpentry, dancing, teaching, business, engineering, etc. (everything else)

This is what we need to add now.

The Sensory Alphabet is the missing alphabet. It is another fundamental symbol system that you'll want your "digital kids" to know and use. Introducing this "alphabet" will multiply your children's repertoire of ways to symbolize and communicate their ideas. And important to the future, it will build the foundation for a more informed interaction with the digital media that uses this symbol system to convey ideas with images, videos, icons, and sound—as well as text and numbers.

Soon, children will need to "speak" image. They will need to be informed creators, not just consumers—with the ability to create infographics with *shape* and *color* to communicate numerical ideas. They will need a working vocabulary of *light* and *sound* to leverage the new technologies that rely on these elements. Digital media uses many forms of communication. Kids have adopted them all. Now they need the foundation of the Sensory Alphabet and the thinking skills of the creative process that will provide jet fuel for their ideas.

A PATTERN LANGUAGE

The Sensory Alphabet: *line, rhythm, space, movement, texture, color, shape, light,* and *sound* make up the patterns our senses take in and to which our brains, instantly and unconsciously, assign meaning and value. When a pattern of qualities—say, *shape* and *color* and *texture*—resonates in a certain way, we recognize a dog or a tree or a vase. So it's not an overstatement to say that we use this sensory vocabulary every single day, every single moment, for everything. Yet often we think of these elements as belonging solely to the territory of the arts or design, and, of course, they are potent tools for creativity in those fields. But if we step back from our usual definitions, it's easy to see how these elements underlie all our perceptions. Every single one.

Rhythm, for example, not only belongs to music but also is basic information to a doctor assessing an electrocardiogram. *Rhythm* is key to devising a spectacular basketball play, a winning debate, or creating a dramatic cinematic moment in the film editing room.

Another example: We might first think of *space* as the tool and consideration of architects, but it's also what tickles the imaginations of physicists and graphic designers—and *space* is very important when you're parallel parking.

The examples are endless.

Some patterns have become emblematic of our culture: the *rhythms* of rock 'n' roll, the amount of conversational *space* between people that can be identified as distinctly western, or the series of *lines* we have come to know as our alphabet. We share these essences and meanings with others in our culture, and when we travel we are often surprised at how other cultures have combined these elements quite differently. Even though the essences and meanings might be similar, our perceptions can be jolted. For example, the amount of conversational *space* acceptable in another culture might, to us, feel threatening, too "in your face." Standard cultural *colors* that are the norm in another culture or region might feel drab to us, or, conversely, too bright.

At a more granular, individual level, there seems to be a built-in sense of what is comfortable when it comes to these elements—certain preferences that come out so early they seem to be inborn. Every parent, especially those who have more than one child, knows this to be so. We all have favorites—certain qualities of *light* or *rhythm*—that are distinctively different from the preferences of other members of our family, certain kinds of *sounds* that are appealing, or a sense of *space* that is "just right" to each person.

These preferences are often expressed unconsciously in the choices an individual makes—for instance, by dressing in favorite *colors,* by demonstrating a love of *texture* with hairstyles or through jewelry or by using big *movements* and gestures again and again. Children express themselves in these ways too. They can tell us their favorites outright, and we can see them in their creative work. These patterns help us, as parents, to identify the unique qualities of each child's imagination. We'll look into individual strengths directly in Part 3.

When children absorb and use this sensory vocabulary on an everyday basis, it becomes second nature. It is easy for them to spot the elements of the Sensory Alphabet. They're close at hand, or eye, or ear. These elements feel welcome to a young mind that has been taught so early the highly abstract forms of the alphabet and numbers. This vocabulary of sensing, comparing, and contrasting is one that every child can master.

And the Sensory Alphabet is inherently *active*. It's the natural foundation for deep interaction with the world. Adopting it builds curiosity and generates ideas. Inhabiting it offers a hands-on, eyes-on, all-senses-on path of discovery and delight. It's like putting on a new pair of glasses!

On the inside, the Sensory Alphabet helps the brain retain a complex and flexible set of connections or pathways, thus helping a child keep his options open. As a child grows, his brain changes—what scientists call neuroplasticity. Brain cells are pruned or enriched according to what happens in the child's environment (Jensen). For example, children are normally born with the physical ability to make the sounds required in all languages. However, from listening to their native language and interacting with the native speakers in their world, their mastery of their mother tongue gradually increases, while the flexibility needed to learn a different language decreases. But involvement with the Sensory Alphabet helps keep those complex connections in the brain developed and fertile. So, a child who routinely plays and creates with *sound* and *rhythm*, in this example, may be expected to learn a second language more easily than a child without these experiences. Keeping neural networks rich and growing gives kids (or adults for that matter) a definite edge for surviving and thriving in today's swiftly changing, global environment.

This "missing alphabet" is the language of sensing and feeling, making and doing. That's why it feels familiar to the arts. But it's the most elemental language of perception, and it is the symbol system *for all forms*—everything that is *out there* can be described by this vocabulary. (Even the alphabet and numbers are made out of *lines!*) It is a way of describing what our senses are telling us and a way of describing anything we make, both tangible and intangible. It focuses on the patterns that underlie our experience.

Because this sensory vocabulary *describes* but doesn't *define*, it expands our capacity to see *patterns*—between disparate objects, fields, and cultures. It opens up our perception. We see differently. We become aware of unexpected relationships that are hidden from us when we define everything we perceive with a label, enclosing the meaning of the "thing" into the boundary of a definition.

When we utilize this vocabulary, our perceptions are more easily mobilized for analysis, comparison, designing, and creating. We are able to give voice to what we perceive in ways that are unburdened by the boundaries, definitions, or prejudices of our culture. We are free to see the deeper patterns of our experience. And this ability to see patterns is one of the hallmarks of a creative mind.

We don't know what children will encounter as they grow up in the next decades, or the problems they will need to solve, or the solutions they will need to invent. We can't anticipate what forms will fill the bill. What we *do* know is that the focus on words and numbers at school is no longer enough to support the array of needs that are becoming apparent now.

What we can do is transform our concern for the future of our children into action by equipping them to be innovators and creators in *any* field. We can offer them the basics that fuel all kinds of minds and appeal to all natural strengths. Within this vocabulary, all kids will be able to find elements that resonate. All kids will be able to say, "I can do that!"

The Sensory Alphabet

It is time to introduce the Sensory Alphabet. What follows is a brief overview of the elements and where we find them in our daily lives. Here, they are described for adult sensibilities, using a more lyrical sense of their qualities and resonances. Notice how they affect you. (In Part 3, we'll discuss them further as we give you practical ways to explore, locate, and put these building blocks together.)

Color

Human vision is distinguished by the color-detecting ability of our eyes. For us, color is often the element of discernment—and the visual language of emotion.

Green with envy, seeing red, walking around under a black cloud—emotion transforms itself into colorful characters, colorful language, poetic passion. Paint on canvas creates sunny weather or an emotional storm; and color in music paints a picture solemn or spritely. Where is your color sense alive? In cooking or chemistry? Stargazing or paint mixing? Finding rainbows, delighting in a feather's iridescence, or in an outlandish and fabulous fashion sense?

Sound

Sound has the inherent quality of acting directly on the emotions without going through the intellect.

Listen. The world is speaking to you in a thousand different voices. When we listen, we put ourselves in the moment: present to an argument, a plea, a whine, a birdcall, the wind in the trees, or a symphony. Besides the obvious (musicians and music), actors, politicians, priests, and parents invoke action with tone, timbre, tempo, and sound. Writers and readers alike listen as words unfurl on the page. Painters may paint a sound, and runners may use one to make the miles fly. Ecologists, anthropologists, birdwatchers, linguists, and physicians all use sound to diagnose, distinguish, and define.

Light

Light delights as the most elusive and changeable element of form: giving contour, creating mood, illuminating all manners of truth.

The sea sparkles, pearls have luster, silk shimmers, we "see the light." Stage designers, cinematographers, photographers, and architects are obvious masters of light and shadow. But think, too, about light as perceived by physicists, glass artists, poets, and urban planners. Without light, we're literally and figuratively "in the dark." Fireflies, fireworks, shadow play, and starlight are some of our first light-filled fascinations—what are others?

Space

Space is omnidimensional, both geographic and temporal, both geometrically present outside of us and metaphorically present inside the fences of our imaginations.

With space, what *isn't* is as important as what *is*: the inside of a basket, the silences between the notes, the pause between the speakers, the room inside the walls. A canvas's size or a room's dimensions determine how we move within it. As humans, we can't help but pay attention to space as space, and space as time. How long? How wide? How fast? How slow? Where and when? Mechanical engineers, publishers, architects, dancers, cartographers, chess players, editors, sitcom writers—how do these people use and analyze space?

Movement

Movement is about change and getting from here to there, from up to down, from then to now.

We talk about how ideas move us, how ambition drives us, how responsibility keeps us tied down, how our imaginations run away, and how our philosophies collide. A story line must move right along or it loses our attention; cycles of days and years and viewpoints become the stuff of history; cycles in our bodies, in weather, and in nature present whole worlds of study. Kinesthetic learners must move into knowledge, often quite literally, finding the meaning of a concept by physically inhabiting it. Movers include (but are not limited to) explorers, botanists, meteorologists, dancers, acrobats, athletes, construction workers, and industrial designers.

Rhythm

Rhythm is the heartbeat element, holding things together in big and little patterns.

We each have a personal rhythm as distinct as our fingerprints, recognizable beneath the changing tides of emotional rhythms that rock and roll us through the day. Rhythm at first thought is audible and invisible—drum beats, finger taps, cadences, and cacophony—but imagine the world without stripes, dots, and dashes, without the visual patterns of steps, of rows of shoes, of the this-way-and-that-way of the lines in a leaf. Without rhythm, who could be a pianist, a mathematician, a poet, an actor, a director, a salesman, a video editor, a debater, a basketball player, a waiter, a politician, an animal behaviorist, or a juggler?

Line

Line, the elemental foundation for print and number, has determined much about twentieth-century life and success in our culture.

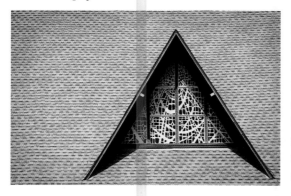

Isobars, arteries, fault lines, line drives, battle lines, lines of credit, timelines, lines of type, notes, and numbers—stretchy, slinky, fixed or floating, dotted or dashed, lines connect two or more points. And the points are, as mathematicians remind us, infinite. Writers pen story lines; programmers, lines of code. Biologists decipher lines of DNA; entrepreneurs develop product lines. Singers follow melodic lines; jazz musicians improvise upon them. Where do you enter the element of line? As storyteller or scribbler? With delight for a maze or an appreciation for ballet?

Shape

Shapes shape other shapes. As shape finders we look for symmetries, for foreground and background, for the doughnut and the hole, for the whole of the thing that is greater than its parts.

Putting puzzles together is playing around with shape, and so is the literary love of beginning, middle, and end. Pleasing shapes play their part in our neighborhoods, our furniture, our plates and platters, our shoes and our cars. Shape-makers include sculptors and typographers; mathematicians with their worlds of symmetries; microbiologists, industrial designers, and couture clothiers. We shape play with shells and rocks, with clay and cookie dough, with big bouncing balls, and smooth, sleek kitty cats.

Texture

At its most direct, tactile information is as close as it gets, up close and personal, right at our fingertips.

Texture is smooth, woven, wrapped, slippery, shiny, course, rigid, and reedy. We *see* texture, too, and *hear* it in a voice or a song. Our days are rough or smooth, our moods even or edgy, our voices piercing or pointed. Surgeons, weavers, gardeners, art collectors, textile designers, and chefs—all must pay close attention to texture. Do you remember exploring texture in the sand box, through a microscope's lens, coiling clay snakes, eating ice cream, or squishing toes in the mud?

THE LANGUAGE OF FORM

As you can see, the Sensory Alphabet is the foundation of all form. In his influential 1967 book *The Medium Is the Massage,* Marshall McLuhan, one of the great theorists of the effects of modern media, predicted the coming of the Information Age and wrote of his concerns:

> *It is a matter of greatest urgency that our educational institutions realize that we now have civil war among these environments created by media other than the printed word. The classroom is now in a vital struggle for survival with the immensely persuasive "outside" world created by new informational media. Education must shift from instruction, from imposing of stencils, to discovery— to probing and exploration and to the recognition of the language of forms.*

As McLuhan predicted, there would be a need for reform in the educational system so that our children could keep up with the changing times. He saw the need for our society to impart that sensory literacy he calls the "language of forms." McLuhan was talking about the Sensory Alphabet.

And just as important as the missing alphabet is the *missing person:* the child, a unique creative potential.

2. The Missing Person

To find the missing person underneath the grades, the competition, the scores, the emphasis on a linear and academic view of what's important, we must be willing to step back for a moment to a broader view of what it means to build a satisfying and successful life—something we all want for our children. This means entering a somewhat fuzzy region that contains *resonance, motivation, intuition, character,* and *identity*—a region that doesn't carry letter or number grades and that counts on parents' discernment.

As a culture, we've focused most all of our educational resources on skills that are more easily measured. But the problem is that, over the years, this extremely academic viewpoint has become a powerful arbiter of a child's identity. Parents have bought into this narrow view of intelligence and future success. To be fair, good teachers have always taken these fuzzier factors into consideration as they try to reach their students. You'll find these concerns are alive and well in discussions in the teachers' lounge and on the coaches' bench.

The good news is that there is now hard evidence that supports the knowings parents have always intuited: There are many different kinds of *smart;* there are many paths to academic goals; and sticking with what you're naturally good at—your individual creativity—boosts motivation, achievement, and productivity (Caine and Caine, 1994; Jensen, 1999, 2001).

HOW WE SEE A CHILD

In our applied research with children over the years at the Learning About Learning Foundation, we have used a sensory lens to discern children's individuality. We offer these tools here as a way for you to analyze the patterns you can discern in your child's work/play and to understand the relevance of what you see. We use the Sensory Alphabet to express both what a child naturally absorbs from the world around him and the characteristics of his uniqueness, his natural expertise—his genius.

For example, a child who loves space, shape, and light may think naturally like an architect, filmmaker, or computer graphics expert. A child who loves line, color, and texture may think best like a poet or designer. Another child who loves movement, rhythm, and sound may have talent as a fine actor or musician. Groupings of these elements can suggest other possibilities too:

space•shape light ☛ architect | photographer | potter

line•color•texture ☛ poet | florist | chef

movement•rhythm•sound ☛ actor | basketball player | songwriter

We have found that when we viewed a child's creative work along with behavioral clues, significant patterns emerge. We describe these patterns using the vocabulary of the Sensory Alphabet and have observed that they do not change over time. Children, now adults, with whom we worked for five, ten, or more years showed surprising consistency in their preferences in the Sensory Alphabet and corresponding products. Here are a few examples of individuals who went into careers that reflected the strengths we could see early in childhood.

Rock—Space, Shape, and Movement

As a young child, Rock was constantly moving through space and exploring its limits—on a skateboard, juggling, climbing trees. He loved simple shapes and constructing with them. His favorite toys were giant-sized dominoes that lent themselves to multiple experiments with space. His sister introduced him to origami and soon he was making the most complex designs and then re-creating them on a large scale. Today he owns several patents for "space-enclosing" devices and systems, and has built, among other things, giant tent shapes that are used for stores, religious services, festivals, and homes.

Johnny—Rhythm

Johnny came from the barrio and, at ten, was a natural leader. He understood how to get his way with people through reading and mirroring the rhythms of their speech and body language. For example, if a teacher started complaining about the mess in the classroom, Johnny would agree with her, using the same rhythm, and suggest they clean the mess together. He often used rhythm to attract people to his way of thinking.

Johnny displayed other indications of his affinity for rhythm: He easily learned to play percussion instruments and invent songs with current rhythms and melodies. He was drawn to complex visual patterns that mimicked the complex aural rhythms he could create so well. Later in life, Johnny followed his rhythm genius to become the top salesman for a copier company, then one of its executives, then his own boss in an entrepreneurial venture.

Cory—Line and Sound

Cory loved the sounds of words and the meanings they made. Before she was of school age, she was creating jokes with her dad using multiple-meaning words, puns, and homophones, like *red* and *read,* and chortling with pleasure. She had a facility for stringing words and their sounds into lines of words and sounds that sometimes expressed a logical argument and at other times, poetry. As a grown-up, Cory was drawn to the world of words and became an editor at a publishing house. Now, as both a writer and an editor, she manages the production of several magazines for a large university.

Rocio—Space

As a little girl, Rocio seemed oddly disconnected—to the degree that had the adults around her a bit worried. One of her teachers, a practicing artist, realized that Rocio saw the world like a surrealist painter. She literally imagined herself on the ceiling looking down at things or peeking at her everyday world from various spatial vantage points. Her teachers introduced her to Remedios Varo, a Mexican female surrealist, and this connection resonated with Rocio immediately.

To help her with math (which she hated), teachers introduced her to the logic/illogic of *Alice's Adventures in Wonderland,* written by Lewis Carroll, a mathematician. Soon Rocio could warm up to math by thinking like Carroll. But her real love was drawing and writing her own books with musings like, "Do I wear my glasses, or do my glasses wear me?" She now practices her art as a photographer, trying out many viewpoints with a camera. Recently, she sent her old teacher some of her images from India.

Kelly—Movement and Rhythm

Kelly is a natural observer and easily thinks like an anthropologist. As a child, when she first came into a new situation, she would most likely imitate the actions and rhythms of those around her, showing little imagination. But, given a little time, she would become the standout in a group.

As it turns out, Kelly learned kinetically by entering into the movement of a new group or person as an observer/learner. Once she mastered the behavior, she used her creativity to invent new kinds of successful interactions. Now she is a Montessori teacher who has learned that system and is creating new curricula and instruction, suited to both her students and the Montessori Method.

Each of these patterns demonstrates how we naturally perceive the world, how we process information, and how we characteristically create meaning. These examples show what we are naturally good at doing. The same qualities of media are chosen again and again—the same qualities of line or the same combinations of colors. And so it is with us all if we take a moment to notice the patterns in our lives. It's no surprise that we call them *favorites.* These choices are where we feel at home, and when we work with our favorites, our imaginations are fluent. These qualities, these favorites are ingrained. These connections have been found consistently in our work with the children we have been privileged to observe and teach for five, ten, twenty, or even forty years at a time.

Let's explore a little of the science that supports why the Sensory Alphabet provides us with the tools needed to identify unique creative characteristics of an individual. We begin with an examination of the sensory filter.

THE SENSORY FILTER

Scientists know that there is more in the environment than can be taken in at once.

Much of the sensory information that is out there at any given time is filtered out. It's all too much for our human perception to handle. So the mind seeks patterns and unconsciously and automatically selects what makes sense and what is personally meaningful. This is known as our *sensory filter*.

An individual's sensory filter is influenced by genetics to some degree but also appears to be quite unique. Parents are aware of this: A child might have inherited Mom's eyes and Uncle David's temper, but she is clearly a different person, more than the sum of these parts. She is an individual all her own—one of a kind.

Every parent knows that each child comes into this world as a unique individual. The things we notice first as parents are these telling traits: a baby who is a mover, full of physical energy, can't be still; a calm baby who needs to sit back and observe everything before joining in; a social baby who loves to engage in interactions with people. These characteristics seem to be indelible as we grow up. How many times have we heard parents recounting tales of their children who were "just like this" from babyhood? And these differences are more far-reaching than temperament or personality. From our long years of working with children, these differences appear to be entwined with patterns in perception, ways of learning, and creating—influences that shape identity.

Other factors besides genes make a difference as well. What a child has learned to believe is important from experience and upbringing—values, prejudices, education, cultural and social norms—all these things help shape what the sensory filter lets in for processing. This all adds up to a singular way of comprehending the world, one that is entirely unique to each child. And it plays out in an equally singular way of decision making, problem solving, and creative thinking.

(For a humorous and accessible look at the sensory filter, read the children's book *Fish Is Fish* by Leo Lionni, and see how the Fish in the story filters information differently than his friend, the Frog, who has a much broader world of experience.)

Neuroscience underscores the uniqueness of each child's brain as well as the myriad ways of thinking and the multiple pathways there are to learning. Not only are brains unique, but they also begin life that way. As John Bransford, professor and author of *How People Learn: Brain, Mind, Experience, and School* (2000), points out, "Even young infants are active learners who bring a point of view to the learning setting . . . An infant's brain gives precedence to certain kinds of information (over other kinds)."

From our perspective, understanding and using all the Sensory Alphabet allows a child to take in more kinds of information and enter into the thinking of people and disciplines (including writers, language analysts, natural and social scientists, and mathematicians) that may be foreign to her natural inclinations.

INDIVIDUAL DIFFERENCES

Over the last forty years, notions of inborn individual differences have been supported by the research of pediatricians, developmental psychologists, and cognitive scientists. The groundbreaking work of Drs. Jerome Bruner, T. Berry Brazelton, and Howard Gardner, among many others, all speak to these issues from the perspectives of their various fields.

Take Howard Gardner's theory of multiple intelligences which came about through extensive scientific research and observation of developing children, brain-damaged individuals, and "geniuses." He proposes at least eight intelligences: *linguistic, logical, spatial, kinesthetic, musical, naturalist, interpersonal,* and *intrapersonal (self-understanding)*. Most all children have the full complement of intelligences in varying degrees (Armstrong, 2009). It is the special combination of these natural differences, in each child, that makes each one as unique as a snowflake.

Knowing teachers take advantage of these natural differences by providing what is called *differentiated instruction*: Each child is challenged to think and learn by starting where they are the strongest (Tomlinson, 1999).

Individual differences, as defined in this book, are not the same as *learning styles*. Educational practices using learning styles commonly assess children as visual, auditory, or tactile/kinesthetic learners and then provide instruction matched to their styles. But, the learning styles model has a specific function: to help diverse learners assimilate the chosen curriculum. In contrast, our aim is to *identify and nurture individual creative strengths*. The learning of any given curriculum is a by-product of this effort and comes about as the child comes to understand and define his own unique way of thinking and learning. Brain

"We all have the same set of systems, and yet all are different. Some of this difference is a consequence of our genetic endowment. Some of it is a consequence of differing experiences and differing environments. The differences express themselves in terms of learning styles, differing talents and intelligences, and so on. An important corollary is both to appreciate that learners are different and need choice, while ensuring that they are exposed to a multiplicity of inputs. Multiple intelligences and vast ranges in diversity are, therefore, characteristic of what it means to be human" (Caine and Caine, 1994, *Making Connections: Teaching and the Human Brain*).

research supports this notion of individuality, as do the studies of multiple intel-ligences (Caine and Caine, 1994; Armstrong, 2009).

Educators and others are beginning to come to grips with what all this research means and how it relates to learning and teaching now. And the implica-tions signal a big departure from the "blank slate" model that is so often the rule in schools today. Most schools only focus on the first two of the eight kinds of intelligences, the *verbal* and *logical* intelligences, and children whose strengths lie in other areas are often left out.

What parents can do is seek out materials, experiences, and even mentors that match and will help nurture their child's unique way of thinking. Although it seems obvious, neuroscience has strong evidence that "people will participate in learning activities that have yielded success for them and avoid those that have pro-duced failure" (Sousa, 2006). Likewise, motivation is strongest when we engage in learning activities for which we have some talent (Gardner, 1999). Going *with the grain* of a child's natural way to learn is most effective to producing profound and long-lasting positive results.

Once again, research tells us that our children (and the rest of us) are hap-piest when in a state of *flow*, which implies mindfulness or focused attention (Csikszentmihalyi, 1990). We can think of flow as being in the zone or in the groove. Flow is a state of total absorption in the activity at hand, and it is the high-est form of intrinsic motivation. We can see flow when a child's work and play seem to merge into a high level of cognitive activity. Flow occurs when the child is doing what he is best at doing and is challenged to operate on a high level. Former teacher and neuroscience scholar Eric Jensen (1999) sums it up in a different way: *"Two rules come from the field of brain research . . . One is to eliminate threat. The other is to enrich like crazy."* These rules are important for parents to remember when creating "work/play" experiences for children that, hopefully, flow.

A child will grow up to choose his or her own career, of course, but to locate areas, early on, where there is a natural resonance can bring real satisfaction, inspire mastery, and unleash deep creativity. And when parents value a child's nat-ural abilities, genuine self-esteem is generated. This becomes doubly important when a child's natural strengths don't match the linear world of schooling. It takes wise and confident parents to support their child's natural strengths, and trust that going with the grain of a child's mind is the most powerful means to equip him for life's challenges.

PREPARING FOR THE FUTURE WORKPLACE

The emphasis we place on individual strengths and patterns of creative potential—on putting the missing person back into the educational equation—takes on an added urgency when we consider the context in which the children of today are developing. One of the very few things that we can project about the future with some certainty is that the rate and scale of change will continue. Undoubtedly, the problems to be solved will be big, complicated, and systemic. These are complex issues, not faced ever before on the planet.

Their solutions will need the ideas of many different kinds of creative minds. They will require systems thinking and collaboration and will be approached by teams of diverse individuals, each bringing their individual strengths, creativity, know-how, and experience to the table—along with an agile mind that can jump the fences between categories and fields of study, over old and now-bankrupt templates.

The forces that have shaped current organizations and educational institutions were informed by a very long history of hierarchical and military thinking, but that is changing quickly now. In his book on the world of work, called *Crossing the Unknown Sea: Work as a Pilgrimage of Identity*, the poet David Whyte peers into the future:

> *The forces that are now shaping our future are being mobilized by the individual imagination. Perhaps, more*

Enriching a Child's Brain

Neuroscience tells us that brain enrichment is important for all kinds of young people, not just those labeled "gifted," and that the windows of opportunity are open widest in the earliest years of life. Researchers have discovered a number of enriching factors that can be adopted by parents and educators alike. Some of the most powerful factors are movement of all kinds and other nonverbal sensory experiences. Exposure to challenging, meaningful, complex, and novel circumstances enriches people of all ages.

To enrich their brains, children need opportunities to observe, play, imagine, explore, respond to, and re-create the world around them—over and over again. Children with enriched experiences demonstrate dozens of successes as they grow—they perform better on cognitive and achievement tests, solve complex problems more readily, show greater emotional development, interact more positively with other people, and, of course, are more creative (Jensen, 2001).

accurately, our future will come from the individual imagination in conversa-
tion with all other individual imaginations. A mobilization of something that
exists at the edges between things. A sea formed not from a general's command
but from the flow and turn of a thousand creative conversational elements.

As the children of today grow up, the call for innovation is growing stronger and more widespread. (Notice its prominence in the 21st Century Education Goals, for example.) We believe the most important education that we can give children today for the workplace of tomorrow is an understanding of, and confidence in, their individual creative potentials. Peter Drucker, the famed "grandfather" of business management practice, agrees. In an interview late in life, he summed it all up: *"The most important thing is to know what you're good at."*

Finding the Missing Pieces

The missing pieces we've presented here are big ones. They represent quite a different viewpoint than the three Rs of today's educational establishment. The idea of adding a different symbol system, another alphabet, along with other thinking skills to the fundamentals that are needed now for children's education may seem radical. And the thought of focusing on individual differences in a classroom setting might appear to be impossible. But, as researchers and educators, we think it's radical common sense. And we've seen it work.

In the last few decades, we've begun to see the dramatic findings of research in the fields of neuroscience and cognitive science. In response to this new knowledge, we must adjust the content of what children learn every day in order to prepare them for a future that is transitioning to a new age based in deep innovation and communication technology. We know now, more than ever, that creativity and imagination are crucial parts of what children need to be able to think critically, solve problems, and find their own strengths—all necessary knowings to be able to participate effectively as thoughtful, tolerant, and creative citizens in the coming global community.

Part 3

The "HOW": Engaging Creativity in the Context of the Everyday

"The possible's slow fuse is lit by the Imagination."
—Emily Dickenson

When looking at creativity, it can be useful to look at it as the sum of various parts—parts that are not alike and that don't necessarily form a sequence. Reading can make a good analogy to get a handle on this idea. Reading as a skill is built up of many different parts and pieces. A few are: the foundation of the alphabet, the fundamental idea that letters of the alphabet make words, the understanding that each word has a meaning, the realization that written words have a spoken equivalent, the left-to-right sweep of the eye across lines of type. Each element is important, yet distinctly different. And it takes all of them together for the phenomenon of reading—understanding ideas from written symbols—to occur.

Creativity is something like that—distinctly different parts that can add up to skillful creative thinking. In the following sections we will focus separately on each element of creativity—*the creative process, the Sensory Alphabet,* and *individuality.* Each element will be defined and enlarged, and we will give you many ideas about how to use them as the basis of everyday activities—to enhance your child's unique creative potential. Finally, we will explore *everyday management of creativity*—how-to ideas for putting it all together and letting creativity happen in the context of our busy days.

Exploring the Creative Process

The creative process is a particular way of thinking and working. But, before we can start exploring the process, we must first consider the vast role of the imagination. The imagination is not exactly a step in the process but the *engine* of the process.

THE IMAGINATION

Imagination is a given. Everybody has one, and it's available 24/7. It constantly fuels ideas for little questions such as "What can I make for a snack?" and big dreams like "What will I be when I grow up?" But, in the past few centuries, the imagination has been underrated and undervalued; we've relied more and more heavily on critical thinking as the thinking process of choice. This bias has fueled mythologies that tend to denigrate the imagination's value and polarize its relationship to critical thinking. (Think of common phrases like "fact or fantasy" as opposites.) Since we're interested in creative thinking, we must rethink and reevaluate the vast role of the imagination. Let's start with a quote from Albert Einstein: *"Imagination is more important than knowledge. For knowledge is limited, whereas imagination embraces the entire world."*

The imagination is like a very deep well. And we don't know where the bottom of that well is exactly. From the depths of those waters, big ideas and little ideas surface in our imaginations all the time. We have clear indications where some ideas come from—maybe from logical thinking or certain areas of expertise or memory. Other ideas pop up quite unexpectedly—"from left field," as the saying goes—perhaps from a dream or a hunch.

When you factor in the notion that we think with all parts of our brain and body, you realize just how much we depend on our imaginations all the time. After all, it's your imagination that's giving you the kinetic idea of how to take a new shortcut to the grocery store, or the visual idea of which socks look right to wear today, or the spatial idea of where you parked in a huge parking lot, or the feeling that a recipe won't work because the batter seems too dry. Most of the work our imaginations do for us goes unnoticed and thus unappreciated.

When we first come into the world as babies, the imagination is going full steam ahead, like a superhighway of intention to all the senses as we take in the blooming, buzzing confusion of our world—looking, tasting, smelling, touching, and opening every drawer that's remotely possible to open. Little by little, however, the imagination gets reined in by parents and caregivers who teach us to follow our cultural blueprint. We are shown when to sleep, what to eat, where to pee, what not to touch, and how to use sound as language. It's called growing up.

Play is the arena where the imagination still reigns. One kind of thinking linked to the imagination is divergent thinking, also known by the corporate cliché: "thinking outside the box." Play is also one way of measuring creativity. Young children typically score very highly in divergent thinking— they are quite familiar with the idea of playing. But when school starts, our society begins to shut the door on the imagination. In its place, we commence teaching and valuing the logical and linear thinking that supports coming up with one right answer. This is called convergent thinking. At this point, scores in divergent thinking begin to diminish significantly. This is not to say that we have no need for the convergent skills that are associated with words and numbers, but convergent thinking is not enough for a present and future where we don't even know the right questions, much less the right answers.

Individual differences in the ways we are wired, first by genes and then by experience, are also associated with the natural brand of imagination we possess. If we are born athletes, we'll always have an inherent connection to movement, and kinetic ideas will flow easily. Likewise, the best ideas of visually oriented people might be in colors, not words. A natural engineer's ideas will be spatial, informed with a clear knowing of what will fit and move and work to solve a problem. We each have some unique mixture of these traits. (More on this in the "Exploring Your Child's Creative Strengths" section.)

We can keep our imaginations filled up and flowing by feeding and exercising them. That means trying out many different kinds of

A note about "ideas" . . . when we use the word *idea,* we mean impulse or notion—not necessarily a full-blown plan.

experiences, using all the senses and exercising the imagination with play. Remember, the imagination is not necessarily partial to words. It loves all sorts of media. Try experimenting by making bread dough, building a tower with marshmallows and straws, balancing on a board, making a light show with gels and flashlights, or designing a treehouse. Play like this on a regular basis, and while you may not remember your experiments the next week, your imagination will become richer and deeper and able to give you even more ideas.

When we apply these ideas to activities we can do with children, we open a world of fun ways to build imagination and "ideational fluency."

The Junk Jar

Here is an example. This is an activity that relies on associative thinking—letting one idea lead to another. It can be for one person alone, or for the whole family as an after-dinner game. Fill an empty gallon jar with tidbits that you find interesting for one reason or another: a feather, shells, old coins, a ribbon, a rock, twigs, buttons, a pinecone . . .

Each person should choose one object. (Parents should step back mentally and notice what each person's choice says about the diversity of the minds around the dining room table.)

- Closely observe your own chosen object.
- Make a list of adjectives that describe your object. Take five or ten minutes to let your mind wander. Consider it as a historian would; then as a scientist would; then a painter, a choreographer, a mapmaker, a sculptor, and any other viewpoint you can imagine.
- Answer these questions: If this object were a time of day, what would that be? If it were a season, what would it be? If it were weather? a machine? a plant? an animal?
- Then, after looking over your whole list of qualities, decide what kind of person those qualities could describe. How old would this person be? What would he look like? What would she be wearing? Name the person. Give this person some history. Decide what your character's biggest concern might be. Think about how this person could have gained the qualities you've written down. Write and draw your ideas.

Now you've used your imagination plus associative thinking to take you from an object to a full-fledged character. Maybe this character could become the star of a short story. If more than one person has been participating, you might take your creations even further. First, share what you've created. Then, let your characters interact. Give them a problem to solve. Develop a story line. You might even decide to write and illustrate your story or make a video. Let your ideas grow and germinate in your imagination. Record new ideas that come to you over the next few days. You'll be surprised at what your imagination will come up with.

CREATIVE THINKING: THE PROCESS

Exercising the imagination leads to the process of creative thinking. The creative process isn't really mysterious; it's a particular way of thinking, like critical thinking or the scientific method. Kids start out doing it naturally and unconsciously. But when you learn and practice this way of thinking consciously, the results are dramatic. It's like having speaking skills and then suddenly adding reading and writing to your repertoire. Creative thinking can turn imagination into jet fuel for ideas and propel grown-up innovation later on.

The thinking processes we all use every day are many and varied. Composing a letter takes a different kind of thinking than designing a doghouse or creating a menu for dinner or making the perfect football play on the fly. Each of these everyday acts of thinking, no matter how conscious or subconscious, draws on the imagination and is manifested in time and space.

Sometimes, thinking processes become formalized and taught to others to achieve specific results. The scientific method is one of these—we make an educated guess, a hypothesis, about an answer to a question. We design an experiment to see if the hypothesis is correct. We repeat our experiment again and again to determine if the results are reliable.

Algebra is another example. While we don't really call it a thinking process, it is a method for solving a problem. Our problem asks us to determine an unknown factor: X. We create equations that include all the factors and quantities we do know in logical relationships. We use the rules and functions of mathematics to solve for X.

Creative thinking exercises *executive function*. Remembering, comprehending, analyzing, synthesizing, and so on are all cognitive functions, i.e., different forms of thinking and learning. Psychologists have learned that there is another kind of functioning, sometimes called *executive* or *metacognitive function*, which is important in coordinating thinking when we are solving problems, searching for the right decision, and otherwise engaged in complex mental operations. These include planning, monitoring, evaluating, and reflecting.

It's as if each of us has a worker and a boss within. The worker does the thinking and learning. The boss looks forward and decides where to begin, monitors what's going on, evaluates progress, and, after work is over, reflects on what happened in order to improve in the future. Playing, interacting with new materials, and otherwise engaging in the creative process exercises these executive functions. For example, in dramatic play, the child is both actor (worker) and playwright/director (boss).

The child may tell himself and others what and how to pretend, and may then proceed to act out the suggested script. Likewise, in creative work, the individual immerses herself in the problem or idea and periodically steps back to see where she has come, where she is going, and where she needs to go next. This immersion and reflection continue until a product or conclusion is reached (Herbert, 1982).

Many everyday activities have a process: cooking, riding a bike, making a budget, etc. Many things you do each day might be so practiced that they seem to happen on automatic pilot. While you may not be aware of it, a series of thinking steps is occurring in your brain to guide your actions. Psychologists call these *scripts* or *cognitive sequences*.

When we learn to do something new, moving through the step-by-step process is a conscious activity. Remember learning how to drive? Putting all the right thinking pieces in the right order is important: Fasten the seat belt, adjust the mirrors, turn the ignition, release the parking brake, put the car in gear, look around, measure space with your eyes, then apply just the right amount of pressure on the pedal with your foot, and so on. It took lots of practice to gain driving expertise over time. Now, however, much of the thinking process for driving has probably become automatic—but you follow the same steps even if you do not consciously notice them.

The creative process of thinking is the same. It's not only a thinking process but also a method of *doing*. And we can learn it just by following the steps. Start by using the creative process consciously, as you would use the scientific method as a young student approaching a science experiment. Let's break the creative process down into its basic components: *collecting, playing, creating,* and *reflecting*.

Collecting

Collecting is about gathering ideas. This can mean both tangibles and intangibles. It could be anything from making a word list of memories to collecting different shapes of seashells. It might include keeping a file of images and quotes that appeal to you or notating dance moves you saw last week on TV.

Collecting is often a neglected first step in the creative process. Many meetings that are hoping for breakthrough ideas start with a "brainstorming" meeting. Brainstorming can be part of the process, but many times few ideas appear because the engine of the imagination hasn't been primed with lots of sensory data input from your collections!

The world is your enormous resource. People watching on the street, cloud shapes recalled from a week at the beach, colors of food you wouldn't like to eat, videos on YouTube, exhibits at the museum, wildflowers on a summer day, textures of fur and the distinctive barks of all the dogs on your block, lists of words that describe a favorite piece of music, memories of Grandmother's attic . . . Draw your ideas from observations, notions, images, materials, feelings. Your collections can contain many media. Why not? They are not formalized, as is an award-winning china collection or art collection. These are bits and pieces of experience that are the raw materials that will nourish your own particular imagination. And this step is just as important and just as true for children as it is for adults.

Playing

As we saw earlier, there are so many ways to play, and in many ways play is at the heart of creativity. When you play, you are combining and recombining bits from your collections, adding other media, spinning "what ifs" and "maybe thens." You are moving from your linear mind into your more intuitive body—and letting your imagination have full reign.

Take play seriously! Neuroscientists and little kids do. The value of play for cognitive, social, emotional development, and well-being is now well documented (Herbert, 2009):

- Play develops empathy and appreciation of diverse viewpoints.
- Play is the beginning of abstract thinking.
- Play improves problem solving and comprehension.
- Play is essential for young children and becomes creative fluency in older children and adults.
- Play is a rich context for developing metacognitive skills.

Everyone knows that it's OK for little ones to play. But by the time kids enter grammar school, play can begin to be a little tarnished and thought of as off task, frivolous, and even useless. It can begin to mean playing around, or fooling around or even messing around. By the time kids are in middle school, the only kind of playing that seems OK is playing sports—or maybe playing video or board games.

We all know the stories of burnt-out kids, children whose lives are structured morning to night with organized sports, lessons in art, piano, language, or what have you, play dates, overnights, and other outings. In the very real life our kids live, it's all too easy to slide down the slippery "something scheduled every afternoon" slope. For one thing, with two active career parents, there's the after-school care quandary. In the city, where many of us live, daydreaming space is at a premium. Raised on three-second sound bytes, fast camera edits, and razor-timed PlayStation modules, kids clamor for more-and-faster media stimulation and often find the endless-summer-firefly kind of time boring.

But time for play—aimless, unstructured, and "unproductive"—is important if you want to build a big imagination for a lifetime of creativity. It lets kids get some distance from everyday reality and deal with ideas instead of actual things and situations. In play, the accent is on creating, from creating characters to making forts, from doodling to climbing. Children can try out ideas, processes, and perspectives that they couldn't or wouldn't in the real world. In imaginative play, there are no consequences! Kids don't have to worry about outcomes or results.

Cognitive experts know that play is thinking in action. Play gives kids a chance to rehearse, direct, invent, imitate, fantasize, try on, try out, experiment, rethink, rearrange, start over, express, and explore—all very important for developing imaginative skills and fluency of ideas. Innovators consistently acknowledge the power of play in their own lives. As parents, we need to allow time for play in the increasingly busy lives of kids and to rejuvenate our own creative thinking as well.

There are endless forms of play. Here are five of them:

"In play a child always behaves beyond his average age, above his daily behavior; in play it is as though he were a head taller than himself. As in the focus of a magnifying glass, play contains all developmental tendencies in a condensed form and is itself a major source of development."
—Vygotsky, *Mind in Society*

1. Play with roles.

Pretend. Pretending lets us imitate something we've seen or read or thought about. It's like trying on an identity. Pretend to be a banker, for instance; try out a banker's thinking by lending "money," counting, evaluating risks and rewards. There's no worry about losing any real money! Or how about a detective? Or a rancher? Childhood is a great time to experiment. Pretending to be a dancer or CEO of a new Internet company or a mommy with a new baby gives a child a sense of what those different roles might be like.

2. Stretch the imagination.
Role play with another person. Adding one or more players stretches the imagination further. Partners in play have to cope with ideas and situations that another person dreams up. When kids play "house" or "pirate ship," it's the imagination that holds up the roof or walks the plank. A version of this kind of activity for big kids might be to create a drama or show with roles and jobs for several people: writing, directing, music, lighting, acting,

set designing, video-recording, editing. This can be a powerful form of play.

3. Play with materials.
Get "hands-on." Joining hands to imaginations makes an important connection. Kids will find that as they play with different materials, the materials start talking back. Children will start having ideas about something else to try—perhaps with a different color or texture or shape . . . or, maybe if they added a feather, then . . .

This kind of play can start a child down an interesting path of exploring and creating.

4. Play in motion.

Get a move on. Stretching and strengthening muscles has its counterpart in the mind. The over-and-over repetition involved in learning to skip rocks, pump a swing, bounce a ball, or jump rope can foreshadow the kind of mastery that later is needed when committing multiplication tables to memory, learning a dance, or writing a business plan. Think of all the ways body language mirrors the qualities we want for an innovative mind: flexibility, strength, quickness, endurance, concentration.

5. Play wild.

Play in the real world. Humans evolved in a wild world. And while finding our way back to the wilderness may not be as easy as it was when just outside the door, children (and parents) instantly respond to even a little bit of wild. Kicking dirt clods, skipping stones on a pond, watching an anthill, wading in running water, lying back in the grass to watch the clouds change shapes—all these activities embody this quality of play. And no, the Disney-ish "nature" of theme parks really isn't the same. Even some city parks have wild corners, and if you live a suburban life, you might find a little bit of wild along your back fence.

Below is a chart of activities designed to take full advantage of the multiple benefits of play:

Benefits of Play	Suggested Activities
Working through difficult problems	Encourage children to express feelings and opinions and simulate tricky problems through puppets and other toys.
Trying out behaviors without the usual consequences	Have children act out their own versions of home and school events.
Learning to see other points of view	Use puppets, masks, costumes, puppets, or props to take on roles of other people. Trade roles with someone and reenact a real or imaginary event.
Developing representational abilities	Use puppets, dolls, action figures, cars, or other objects to stand for and act out people, animals, and things. Mimic interactions in the everyday environment. Use dramatic play to visualize story problems in math.
Developing divergent thinking	Use everyday objects for imaginative play. How many things can you do with these: a piece of cloth, a long cardboard tube, a pencil, a block, a box, etc.?
Developing creative abilities	Invent and act out unique stories and puppet creations and other characters.
Promoting conceptual understanding	Play with the meanings of words like "run" or "draw." Brainstorm examples or possibilities.
Developing cause/ effect thinking	Play with the notion "What would happen if . . . ?" Create scenarios and play them out. For example, "What would happen if everything was the same color?" or "What would happen if steel disappeared?"
Understanding sequences of action	Invent add-on stories, perhaps using puppets. Have one person start the story, then another take it up. Act out the main sections of narratives you read.
Developing social skills	Use props and puppets in imaginative play centers to encourage interactive play. Play board games and sports.
Developing metacognitive skills	Let children engage in free play with a partner. Have pairs report what they played. Have individuals report what they like to play and why.

Media: Bringing ideas into the world.

As we think about play, it also important to consider *media* and its pivotal role in the creative process. Using media is how you get ideas from inside your head out into the world. From a song, to a dance step, to an essay—it's not only the way to make an idea apparent to your own senses but also to communicate ideas to others. And the choice of media matters.

When you hear the word media today, it usually connotes some kind of journalism, meaning newspapers, magazines, or television. Media used this way most often means "mass media," some form of information designed to reach many people at once. And the term has also become paired with "digital" to designate the many technological means for sharing information. But the original meaning of the word media comes from the same Latin word *media,* and it's the plural form of the word. The singular form is *medium*; two or more "mediums" make *media.* It originally meant "in between" or "the middle." For instance, the Latin phrase that's used sometimes in our legal documents, *in media res,* means "in the middle of things."

In fact, the medium *is* in the middle of things. The medium is whatever material you use to make an idea apparent to the senses. If you're talking, the medium consists of spoken words that make your ideas apparent to someone else's ears. If you're giving directions to someone, the medium could be spoken words or written words. Or the medium might be drawn lines on a piece of paper: a map. A mathematical idea is most often expressed through the medium of numbers. You get the idea.

You use many media every day to get your ideas and your messages across—consider making a chart of media that you are familiar with and use often. You will soon realize that some media are better than others for the job. Take, for example, the problem of giving your friend directions to the zoo. You could give her verbal directions, using spoken words to tell her how to get there. You might even use your hands to give her more information, using movement to show how the road curves just a little to the right.

But you might want to write the directions down with words, noting the landmarks she'll pass on the way. Or you might give her a printed map. The tiny lines and words on that map give lots of information about distance, direction, and way-finding. But what if you're standing outside with nothing to work with and no map in your pocket? You might draw a map in the dirt with your finger. Your dirt map might be able to get a rough idea across, but you won't have the same amount or kind of information that the printed, colored lines have.

So, the important thing here is this: The medium that expresses an idea or a message has a big effect on that information. It shapes the idea, emphasizing certain aspects and diminishing others. An effective media choice will produce a strong impact, like a good ad. Or it could be faint, like a whisper in the wind. When you are choosing your medium of expression and are conscious of its possible effects, you're more in control of the message. And the more media you are familiar with, the more ways you have available to express your ideas. It's just common sense.

There's another interesting quality about media you happen to choose. When you really get into playing with it, when you really give your attention to the medium you're using, it begins to talk back. It begins to give you ideas. Experts in any field would agree. As the carpenter works with wood, his imagination gains depth, and what he can create and predict about what is possible with wood grows. The same idea holds true with cooks and food, physicists and numbers, clothing designers and fabrics. The list is infinite.

Following this line of thinking, common sense also tells us that we want our children to experience many media—pounding and shaping clay, beating drums and blowing whistles, singing and whispering, mixing paint and mixing batter, turning cartwheels and dancing, drawing with thin pen lines and also fat brushes, writing poems and writing essays, braiding hair and twisting rope, building with blocks and building with sand.

Here are more media ideas: Draw with water on the sidewalk, oil paint on boards, colored inks on tissue paper, icing on a cake, or chalk on the playground. Paint with sponges, sticks, rubber stamps, old toothbrushes. Sculpt with homemade playdough, clay, twigs, paper clips, wood scraps. What would happen if you sewed together really big paper shapes with yarn and stuffed them with wadded-up newspaper? Built a city out of milk cartons? Made a thirty-foot creature out of sand at the beach? Filled up an empty room with stretched strings and masking tape to create new spaces?

Playing and getting familiar with many media creates a deep well of resources for children to draw from to embody their ideas. These experiences fill the imagination (though not necessarily consciously) and give children more ideas, more flexibility, and more power to communicate their ideas.

Parents play a key role here. If parents value and support a child's beginning work/play in various media—whether it's cooking, drawing with chalk on the sidewalk, or building a hamster house with recycled materials—the child will take away the knowing that other things and other senses are valued in their world, not just winning competitions and earning high test scores.

Creating

The act of creation is where you begin to select, add, shape, edit, and polish—taking your ideas and giving them form. This could be as simple as a sandwich, or as big and complex as a symphony. It involves the somewhat magical mixing of your collection of ideas, the inspiration that comes from the imagination, your collection of ideas, the experiences you and/or your body remembers of the media you have chosen, and the analytical part of your mind.

It's like a dance. Now up close, experiencing that focus where you can lose yourself between your ideas and the materials you're working with (hopefully experiencing "flow")—then stepping back to observe what's happened, asking "did it work?" and operating with your best critical thinking to evaluate, edit, add, decide what to do next. Now up close again, to work in the world of media—now back, to get the big picture. This is the dance of creation.

Ask for creative work from your children. Put out some "scratch" materials (whatever resources are handy), and present a problem to solve that is appropriate for the developmental stage of the child. It might be place cards for dinner, a "surprise" game for a toddler, an organizer for the back of the seat of the car, or a new cover for the phone book. It might not be something "useful." How about a sound machine, the most interesting digital photo that shows "speed," or a paper doll dress from the best color of pink in six magazines?

Share the steps of the creative thinking process with children who are old enough to get it. It can be really helpful for a child to know that *collecting ideas* is separate from *creating/making* and deserves time and attention all its own. Lead the younger ones. Be patient with the process. Allow plenty of time for the collecting and playing part.

Then let creating happen. The result won't be what you would have done, no doubt. It may not be exactly what would solve the problem best. But consciously exercising the process is worth the time and effort. It's like reading: It takes time and practice. And adults help children along by presenting an interesting challenge at the right time.

When a child is ready for a more sustained experience with the creative process, making "a study" is a valuable way of working with ideas. A study is an investigation of a single thing, theme, or idea. In a study, a child explores many, many different viewpoints, contexts, and materials. After much investigation, the child expresses a personal definition or viewpoint through one or more forms—that is, she creates! This kind of creating can be more complex and refined, and worthy of more reflection.

For a child, or any of us, to be able to use a concept to solve problems, make decisions, express ourselves, and enrich our quality of life, we need a well-elaborated concept—one that looks like a very complex spider web of interconnected experiences and ideas. The study makes this an overt process and leads toward deep understanding and transference of that understanding into many new contexts—what has been called the "so what?" of learning.

The following pages give you some specific ideas for engaging in the creative process with your child.

A STEP-BY-STEP GUIDE FOR PARENTS THROUGH THE CREATIVE PROCESS

Making a Study

(Note: For children younger than seven, studies should be of short duration. Older children can spend weeks or even months on a single topic.)

To put this process in concrete terms, here is an exercise using different materials and different starting ideas to take you and your child through the process together. One of the truths about this process is that the more the original idea is interesting and intriguing to the child, the more it is something he or she can sink teeth into, the better the process works. The next few pages illustrate a simple study with specific content and a specific format direction. The payoff for your child will most likely come when you set up a study that honors a subject your child is passionate about—maybe even obsessed with.

Put yourself—the grown-up—in the supporting cast, follow your child, and let his or her ideas and natural inclinations lead the process. Remember that these are just jumping-off places for an investigative study. As you and your child—or your child alone—work through some of these exercises, you may decide to change the rules in midstream, following one idea that pops up into a totally unexpected form of its own. The magic of an idea-to-form process is, indeed, its very nonlinear and unpredictable nature. By learning to pay close attention along the way, throughout the process, children learn to find the "right" form, the best and most fitting form for their ideas. As parents mentoring this process, we can best support it by providing the tools and materials that are called for, by acting as a supportive audience that pays attention and provides feedback, and by getting out of the way and letting the child have a go at it.

An Example: Making a "Favorites" Study

Step 1: Collecting ideas.

Start a conversation about favorites and look for them in everyday spaces. Share yours and find out your child's. Starting points include favorite clothes, favorite shoes, favorite window view, favorite tree, favorite place to hide, favorite words, favorite dance, and then, using the Sensory Alphabet as a jumping-off point, consider favorite colors, textures, shapes, spaces . . .

Ask your child to draw, using markers or colored pencils or watercolors, simple sketches and painting impressions of these favorites. Label these with appropriate narrative: "My favorite blue hat," "A favorite line," "My favorite space for naps." Cut or tear pictures from magazines or take digital photos and print them. The goal: to compile a good collection of all kinds and categories of favorites. Or you can concentrate on just one category, such as favorite colors.

Step 2: Playing with an idea—a.k.a. "brainstorming."
Ask your child to pick his or her most interesting or most intriguing idea about favorites from the bigger collection, just compiled—it could be one idea with several categories, such as favorite colors, or a single favorite thing. Try the following playful approaches to generate even more images and information. With younger children you can have a "what if" conversation to play with the ideas and then encourage your child to draw, write, or otherwise record the ideas and images that come to mind. With older kids, you might even make up a study notebook of envelopes (for small collection pieces and experiments) and blank pages for him to use to chart the process.

Examples with a favorite color include:

- *Make it bigger.* What if everything in the world was your favorite color? What if your favorite blue hat was big enough for you to live inside? What if your favorite space was big enough for a hundred of you?
- *Make it smaller.* What if you had only a tiny piece of paper with a tiny splash of your favorite color—and no one else had ever seen this color? What if your favorite blue hat could be worn by an ant? What if your favorite space was big enough for you, but only if you were the size of a peanut?
- *Look at the opposite.* What is the opposite color of your favorite color? Why do you think so? What would happen if everything in the world were painted this color? Could your favorite blue hat be turned into blue shoes? What if everyone wore blue shoes? What are the qualities that describe your favorite space—what are the opposite qualities and what kind of space would they make? How would you feel in this opposite kind of space?
- *Change your viewpoint.* Tell the life story of your favorite color: "I am green . . . I live in a . . . I eat . . ." Draw pictures of your favorite blue hat from every perspective, above, below, close to, from far away, through a microscope. Draw a map of your favorite space as though it were a city, a playground, a country all its own.

- *Make a match.* Match your favorite color to these categories: food, sounds, times of day. Imagine adding the following to your favorite blue hat: feathers, strings, giraffe head, water, fruit. What if your favorite space was also filled with your favorite textures? Imagine your favorite space matched to these inhabitants: an alien, a dinosaur, a ferocious lion, a tiny pet.
- *Add other elements.* Literally, or in your mind's eye, explore your idea favorites consciously using the language of invention: the Sensory Alphabet. What happens when you add your favorite color to different textures? What happens to your favorite space in different kinds of light? What if that favorite blue hat was transformed into a hundred different shapes?

Step 3: Creating—moving from synthesis to form.
By this time more than one of these ideas will have started to sprout wings. An attentive parent can help guide the process by providing feedback and help with selection and matching to age- and skill-appropriate materials and media. The results of the study may now be turned into a homemade book or other form. Younger children can simply select and organize sketches and transcribed stories into a notebook or scrapbook. Older children may want to tackle making a simple handmade book. There are many other decisions to make along the way that will affect the final look and style of the book, including the kind of illustration materials (colored pencils, markers, oil pastel drawings, watercolors, cutout or torn paper collage, digital photos or snapshots, etc.). Experiment with a variety of media.

Other suggestions for making a homemade book include the following:
- Arrange ideas into different kinds of categories.
- Make a connected story with a selection of ideas.
- Put sketches and words into a template of grids or columns.
- Try a Japanese folding book format.
- Design a page or two in different formats of size and shape to check out how the final form will look.
- Make a "thumbnail layout," i.e., a rough draft of tiny pictures of each page so that you see how the whole book will flow before you fill out each page.

Step 3.5: Polishing your creation.
Sometimes a child will want to stop with step 3. Other times, she will want to go further. For a presentation to an audience, almost any innovative effort can benefit from a bit of polish. Including this as a conscious part of the invention of a form gives children experience in mastery. Sometimes, a bit of parent-furnished polish gives children's work the presence it needs to help the child see his or her own idea's

excellence. Sometimes, an adult's helpful technical skills or better-developed motor skills are needed to make a form shine. Straight lines are sometimes called for.

With word forms, you may want to help your child make sure the spelling and grammar are correct to keep the communication clear. With illustrations, kids can "clean up" their work by gluing final illustrations onto clean, bordered sheets, erasing pencil guidelines, etc. Polishing gets more sophisticated with age, but we think that kids' work deserves to be treated with respect. Sometimes, a project that has taken more effort and time—such as the one described in this study process—will deserve more than a temporary home on the refrigerator door. The finished product may become part of a homemade family library, available to inspire new creative projects in the future.

Step 4: Reflecting.
Reflect on the process with your child. As a step in making a study and as an important part of the creative process in general, *reflecting* involves looking back over all the ideas that were collected but not used this time—the experiments with materials that provided ideas about others to try, themes and favorites to expand on later with new idea additions or new materials.

Ask your child what parts of the process she liked the best and what she learned about herself. Notice choices your child made (or rejected) and ideas that sparked smiles. Mull things over. Take notes. Make plans for jumping-off points for next time. This part of the process is for you both to share with your child and to do all alone. Together, let your imaginations wander down the path of *what ifs* and reflect on other materials, sizes, timing. What questions or new ideas come to mind? Does this experience generate a "Let's try this next time"?

Building in habits of reflection helps young inventors step back to see a bigger, more analytical picture that can help build creative momentum. For parents, you can enjoy knowing that all the experiments and original ideas will be tucked away in the back pocket of a young imagination, to be sorted and resorted, maybe taken apart and remembered in some new, likely hidden way, by a growing and evolving mind at work.

Reflecting

As a key element in the creative process, the step of reflection offers the opportunity for a change of viewpoint and direction. The high focus on what's being created, made, or composed can be relaxed. It's time to stop and take a breath. The energy that has been flowing outward toward the object of creation can reverse directions, flow inward, and take a broader view.

Whatever has happened, your creation can now be a source of information, a source of surprise, even a source of wonder. Stand back and be open to its effects. Ask questions. Look. Listen. Invite the muse to whisper in your ear. Reflect on your creation. Reflect on yourself as creator and your process. Give time to this often forgotten part of creative work. You'll likely be surprised at what bubbles up — new content ideas, new media ideas, intriguing combinations that you wouldn't have imagined before.

After a while, reflection gives way to a new inspiration and intention. And that intention circles back around to collecting. A new beginning—and you're off down a new path!

Exploring the Sensory Alphabet: A Field Guide

Almost anything—any place, any piece of art or work of music, even an idea—can be experienced through any one of the elements of the Sensory Alphabet. Each of the nine "letters" is like a new and different pair of glasses. For example, a tree can be seen through the lens of *line* (the branches, the roots, the veins on the leaves), *texture* (the bark, the foliage against the sky), *color* (leaves in different seasons, branches and bark), *movement* (in the wind, inherent in the tree's structure), etc.

Some things—specific tools and materials, certain places and experiences—are particularly suited to collection, exploration, and invention within one particular sensory alphabet lens. A ballet performance or an older sibling's soccer game offers you and your child opportunities that are custom-built for watching, analyzing, and talking about *movement* and *rhythm*—before, during, and after the excursion. Big pieces of paper, chalk, and large wax crayons give young children the perfect tools for exploring *texture* as they make rubbings of sidewalks, pebbled walls, metal embossed signs, and other everyday surfaces around the house or on a neighborhood walk with you. People watching as you wait for the grocery checkout can be a great time to try on the *shape, space,* and *rhythm* lenses.

In Part 2, you were introduced to each of the nine elements. This section includes a more specific description of each element, including photographs to share with your child (and to inspire your own collections), quotes from famous people that illustrate diverse experiences of a particular element, a vocabulary to jump-start a lexicon of words and ideas, and activities matched to different experiences and environments. You'll also find a list of suggested "scratch" materials and digital tools, possible plans for excursions and recommendations of artists, writers, scientists, and other creative people whom you and your child might like to meet through stories, movies, or exhibitions. You'll see how these elements can be used at different stages of the creative process—for collecting; for playful exploration; to create, edit, and refine; and while reflecting on the products of an investigation or study.

Parents, take note: Many, if not most, of these activities can be integrated into everyday routines, ordinary chores, and ongoing actions: going to the grocery store, waiting in the pediatrician's office, a trip to the park, or a walk around the block. We don't want to add more "things to do with your child"; it's clear that parents of young children already have their plates full. Rather, this field guide is designed to help you *make the most* of the time, experiences, excursions, and opportunities that you already share with your child. These activities and the tools and materials that we suggest are also designed to help you select toys, tools, and "stuff" that add to, rather than dampen, your child's innate creativity. We've made suggestions for some specific projects in specific places, but once you've mastered the alphabet, you'll find that the sensory alphabet lenses become second nature.

Line

Line

Range

Line is literally linear. A line goes from one point to the next. Lines are apparent through your eyes, ears, nose, feet, and muscles, and through your sense of direction.

Description

Lines have a trajectory that may be straight or curved, zigzagging or looping, undulating, jagged, bumpy or smooth, twisted, dotted or continuous. We see lines in tree branches, window grids, maps, faces, and the strata of rocks.

We *hear* lines in music, in dialogue, in poetry, and in "lines" of reasoning. We experience waiting in line, lining up, aiming at a target, stretching a muscle, crossing or towing (or even toeing) the line. We learn about number lines and story lines, lines of access, delineation, and of direction; borderlines and boundaries between people, places, nations, and cultures. We can trace our family lineage or place important dates on a timeline.

Lines connect a beginning to a middle to an end, whether in space, time, or the imagination. Lines make shapes when they connect, textures when they overlap or interweave.

Connections

- Draftsmen describe buildings, roads, and realities that are yet to come.
- A mapmaker uses lines to show elevation and to connect roads, rivers, and railways.
- Writers must craft a story line to make sense and to impose meaning from beginning to end.
- An actor interprets a play's or film's script with the lines of his body, speech, face, and expression.
- Scientists and mathematicians express formulas and analyze data with lines of code, lines on graphs, and lines of reason.

The Key Question

What connections do lines make in your life, between ideas, and in the time and space around you?

Looking for Line

Materials and objects for exploring and playing with line

- string, yarn, and wire
- large paper (such as butcher paper rolls) and narrow paper (such as adding machine tape)
- Japanese calligraphy brushes and India ink
- storybooks
- nails and boards for weaving frames
- simple looms, such as a kitchen hot-pad loom or a pin loom
- cartoon books with linear drawings and story lines
- calligraphy pens
- blackboard and chalk, or whiteboard and markers
- different drawing and writing implements, such as broad and narrow point markers, drawing pencils, pens, and charcoal sticks
- maps and graphs
- letters and sentences
- stringed instruments
- Spirograph toy
- strings and pinboards to make string art—see http://www.mathcats.com/crafts/stringart. html; http://en.wikipedia.org/wiki/String_art; http://www.emagu.es/index.php/galeria-de-cuadros (a gallery of string art by Spanish artist Emagu)
- Zen Brush, an app for phones and tablets—the digital equivalent of a calligraphy brush with different brush sizes, papers, and opacities of lines
- TypeDrawing, an app for phones and tablets—turns words, phrases, and sentences into linear patterns and designs

Line

Talking about Line

What is straight? A line can be straight, or a street, but the human heart, oh, no, it's curved like a road through mountains. —Tennessee Williams

When I came from horizontal vertical straight all old stuff then suddenly I go also again in curved lines. And there I submit to changes in the intensity of my hand leading a tool, you see. —Josef Albers

The idea is to write it so that people hear it and it slides through the brain and goes straight to the heart. —Maya Angelou

I realized by using the high notes of the chords as a melodic line, and by the right harmonic progression, I could play what I heard inside me. That's when I was born. —Charlie Parker

A line is a dot that went for a walk. —Paul Klee

It's a little like casting out hundreds of fishing lines into the audience. You start getting little bites, then more, then you hook a few, then more. Then you can start reeling them in and that's the loveliest feeling—the whole audience laughing with you. —Jim Dale

Line at Home and In Your Neighborhood

Collect Line
- Listen to different kinds of music. Can you hear lines of sound in the melodies and rhythms?
- Collect lines in your neighborhood or front yard with a digital camera or markers on paper.
- Find as many kinds of sticks, string, yarn, and wire as you can in your home and yard.
- Look for lines in buildings, in nature, and in everyday places and objects.
- Make rubbings of the lines you find in manhole cover designs and other embossed images on the street.
- Look inside a piano or a guitar while it is being played.

Play with Line
- String a ball of yarn around your house or outdoors and have someone follow it to the end.
- Listen to music together and talk about the melody and rhythms you hear. How could they be drawn as lines? Make the lines you hear with your hand and arm, or dance them with your body. Draw the lines on paper with markers or ink and brush.
- Make simple stringed instruments with rubber bands, boxes, cans, wire, and other simple materials.
- Draw happy, sad, mad, and scared lines with paint, markers, or pastels. How does the line change with the emotion?
- Draw your own cartoons.

Select, Create, and Make Line
- Find out about your family history. Make a family tree with photos and stories about all the people in your "line."
- Make a timeline of a period of history that is interesting to you, or for a fictional story or series of stories. Tape a large sheet of butcher paper to the wall or several walls around an entire room. Add the key events, people, and ideas showing the sequence in which they happened. For inspiration, see this video that shows an imaginative and colorful view of evolution: *Big Bang Big Boom* by BLU, at http://vimeo.com/13085676.
- Using index cards and photos from magazines (and/or from your child's life), make story cards that can be rearranged to tell different story lines. Arrange them in different ways to tell different stories to one another.
- Play exquisite corpse, a group storytelling game. One person starts a story with a sentence; each person adds to the story in turn around the circle. This game was invented by the Surrealists around the beginning of the twentieth century; the name was part of a nonsensical phrase "the exquisite corpse will drink the new wine."
- Plan, prepare together, and eat a "line" meal, with spaghetti, string beans, shredded cabbage or coleslaw, pretzels in different shapes, string cheese, and for dessert, licorice laces or ice cream with squirted toppings.
- Explore the sounds that stringed instruments can make. Make up a simple song on the guitar, piano, or ukelele.

Line

Line at the Zoo

Collect Line

- Look for lines in the animals you see and in the zoo environment. Collect lines with a sketchbook and marker or with a digital camera.
- Using a map of the zoo, plan the "line" of your visit before you visit different sections. Trace the path of your line with your finger or a marker on the zoo map. When you get home, draw your own map of your visit.
- Compare these lines on various animals: the line of the neck, moving legs, stripes, how the animal moves in its confinement. Could you draw a map of all the lines about one animal?

Play with Line

- Here is another version of the exquisite corpse game. Each person around a circle starts with a piece of paper, drawing one line as part of an animal and then passing the paper to the next person. See what silly animals you can invent, and make up a story about each animal. You can do this when you get home, or even at the zoo, passing around one sketchbook as you visit different animals.
- When you look closely at an animal, see how many line words you can use to describe the way it looks and behaves: *striped, skinny, long, wide, wavy.*
- Make the body lines of the animals you see by tracing them in the air or posing your body in the same lines.

Select, Create, and Make Line

Back at home, use the ideas and images you collected at the zoo for one or more of these line projects:

- Using brushes and paint, make giant line drawings on really big paper of the animals you saw. For more inspiration, look at pictures of prehistoric cave drawings and aboriginal art from Australia.
- Turn your zoo experience into a skit or story, with amazing story lines and adventures that happen in the zoo.

Line at the Art Museum

Collect Line

- Use the art museum as a site for a line scavenger hunt, collecting lines with a digital camera or sketchbook.
- Using line words, talk about the artwork you see. How did the artist use lines to make the painting, sculpture, or other artwork more interesting?
- Tell a story about a painting you see, including a beginning, a middle, and an end.

Play with Line

- Translate the lines you see in a painting or sculpture into movement you can do with your arm and hand.
- Back at home, use a postcard of a piece of art that you saw to inspire a wire sculpture or a line drawing.
- Make line drawings and wire sculptures with different art materials and decide which ones you like best. Which materials make the most interesting lines?
- Explore computer games and software features that use lines for drawing and as photo filters (changing a photograph to a line image). Some to try are the "Outline" filter in Adobe Photoshop, Google SketchUp (free) http://sketchup.google.com/download/, and Art Pad at http://artpad.art.com/artpad/painter/. Use the inspirations and photos you took from your museum visit to play around with line with these and other digital tools.
- Another artistic site is Plasma Tree, at www.openrise.com/lab/PlasmaTree.
- Scribbler, http://www.zefrank.com/scribbler/gallery/index_ran.html, is also a generative illustration tool, just one of a number of intriguing interactive toys by Zefrank.

Line

Select, Create, and Make Line
- Back at home: Many simple "how to" drawing programs are available on the Internet. If your child really likes line drawing, find a site that is appropriate for his or her age. SQUIDO.COM offers user-created content with several links to drawing tools and games.
- Try contour drawing with your child: Choose something interesting to draw. Looking only at the object and not at your drawing, move your pencil *slowly* on the paper and see what happens. Pretend your eye is the pencil moving around the contours of the object. This is an interesting approach to drawing pets and people, too.
- Look at the wire circus sculptures by artist Alexander Calder (a video tape is available also at http://www.youtube.com/watch?v=t6jwnu8Izy0). Help your child make his or her own wire sculptures.

Special Activity: Line in Maps and Charts_____
Collect Line
- Collect and look at different kind of maps and graphs that use line—as many as you can find—on the Internet, in magazines, at the gas station, at the library.
- Make photocopies and tear clippings from magazines and newspapers as you create a physical collection of maps, informational graphics, and charts. If possible, make a giant map and chart wall in your child's room, collaging your collection on a wall-sized pinboard or a bulletin board (you can make one with insulation board or corkboard tiles).

Play with Line
- Find and learn to use Internet mapping and charting software apps and sites that are appropriate for your child's age.
- Make a "plan view" version of your neighborhood by drawing a map on large paper on the floor or taped to the wall. If you wish, this can be the pattern for a painted floor cloth or wall mural.
- Work on map puzzles.
- Look at different kinds of globes.
- Investigate migration maps for birds and insects.
- "Play" the New York City Metropolitan Subway at this site: http://www.mta.me/.

Select, Create, and Make Line
- Draw a map of your neighborhood, including roads, creeks, houses, and important features. Remember to use an "overhead" view as your starting point. You can look at an enlarged map on the Internet (at Yahoo Maps, Google Maps, or Google Earth) to get the streets in the right place! (Be sure to look at the satellite view, too.)
- Make a "map" of your child's typical week or day, using pushpins to stretch strings between different activities and places.
- Learn to make "mind maps" with your child to explore ideas and make studies. Resources for mind mapping can be found online with a free trial of iMindMap by Tony Buzan, or FreeMind, a free open source downloadable program. Many other mind mapping apps and programs are available, too. For research that uses a mind mapping format, look at Wikinodes, a tablet and cell phone app.
- Mind-mapping on paper, however, is easiest of all.

Reflect _____
- Of all the line activities you tried, which ones were your child's favorites?
- Do you think your child has a special affinity for linear thinking, linear patterns, storytelling, or logical reasoning?
- Could your child benefit from communications, routines, and daily structures that are clear, ordered, and organized with a sense of line?
- How does your sense of line match or not match that of your child?
- Where and how and when in your family's everyday life could attention to line make a difference in the quality of time you spend together?

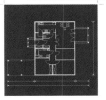

Line: Field Notes

Write | Paste | Draw

Rhythm

Rhythm

Rhythm Words

walk, run,
gallop, jump,
saunter, skip,
stomp, swing,
meander,
undulate,
leap, sneak,
hiccup, yawn,
giggle, yap,
blink, gossip,
chatter, tiptoe,
doze, beat,
tempo, time,
staccato,
adagio,
largo, allegro,
nervous,
jittery, busy,
calm, slow,
antics, habit,
routine, ritual,
rut, holiday,
celebration,
rhumba,
waltz, tango,
hip-hop,
march,
rock 'n' roll

Range _____

Found often beneath the surface, rhythm occurs through time and space. Visual and aural expressions are ubiquitous.

Description _____

Rhythm is a close cousin to patterns: of movement and sound, of shapes in space, of lines of waves. You can't have one (that is, "rhythm") without the other (that is, "pattern"). Movements may have rhythms of marching, swaying, galloping, strolling, pacing, jogging, rolling, skipping, hopping, or bouncing. Sounds may be percussive, steady, syncopated, staccato, rising and falling, speeding up and slowing down, boom–boom–boom. You can see rhythm in stripes and stars, arches and curves, dots and wiggles, concentric and interlocking patterns.

Machines, animals, and people march to their own rhythms with sounds and movement, in space and time. Sometimes rhythms are monotonous, other times upbeat, persistent, sneaky, or calming. We can hear rhythms in poems, songs, arguments, gossip, greetings, games, and sermons. Rhythms are the changes in viewpoint, movement, and sound from start to finish in a movie. Rhythm is what keeps a song in our head, and what keeps us turning the pages of a book.

The big rhythms of the earth and universe keep on turning through our lives: ocean waves, gravity's pull, magnetic pulses, heartbeats, brain waves. At the big and little ends of our perception, you'll find rhythm.

Connections _____

- A drummer's work is all about rhythm.
- Scientists, mathematicians, and artists all work with and seek grand patterns (rhythms) in the universe.
- Biologists are concerned with cyclical, seasonal, and other rhythms of growth and decay.
- Meteorologists study weather rhythms in order to predict and understand the cycles of wind, air, water, and earth.
- Dancers move to internal and externally counted rhythms, even when they don't hear music.
- Many kinds of everyday work rely on establishing a rhythm: ironing, digging, hammering, typing . . .
- Good directors, screenwriters, movie editors, and cinematographers work with the rhythm of the story, the camera, the scene.
- Actors, psychologists, and social workers must all have the ability to read and interpret emotional and physical rhythm information—to know what is going on behind and beyond speech.
- Poets master rhythm as a tool of expression.

The Key Question _____

How do you notice and use rhythm to get work done, to stay the course, to change a temper tantrum into something better?

Looking for Rhythm _____

Materials and Objects for Exploring and Playing with Rhythm

- drums and percussion instruments
- materials to make shakers and rattles
- stickers and dots (to use on adding machine tape to notate rhythms)
- digital camera (preferably one that can shoot video)
- calendars
- people to watch
- animals to watch
- poetry books
- chants, jump rope rhymes, hand clap games

Rhythm

Talking about Rhythm

Almost all American white people at that time seemed to think that all Negroes could sing and dance and that all of us had a sense of rhythm. So I came to the conclusion that maybe poetry, rhythm, color, me a Negro, that little boy had thought he must have some rhythm to give a poem, and maybe that's why I was elected the class poet. Anyway I'm glad that I was. —Langston Hughes

A book is a part of life, a manifestation of life, just as much as a tree or a horse or a star. It obeys its own rhythms, its own laws, whether it be a novel, a play, or a diary. The deep, hidden rhythm of life is always there— that of the pulse, the heartbeat. —Henry Miller

The drum is sacred. Its round form represents the whole universe, and its steady beat is the pulse, the heart, throbbing at the center of the universe. —Nick Black Elk

When we experience a film, we consciously prime ourselves for illusion. Putting aside will and intellect, we make way for it in our imagination. The sequence of pictures plays directly on our feelings. Music works in the same fashion; I would say that there is no art form that has so much in common with film as music. Both affect our emotions directly, not via the intellect. And film is mainly rhythm; it is inhalation and exhalation in continuous sequence. Ever since childhood, music has been my great source of recreation and stimulation, and I often experience a film or play musically. —Ingmar Bergman

Rhythm at Home and In Your Neighborhood

Collect Rhythm

- Take a "rhythm walk" around the block or around the playground; follow the leader adding different rhythms to your walk. With older children, take your cue from the people you see on your walk.
- Make a collection of rhythms from family lore with your child: the counting rhymes your parents knew; jump rope, hand clap, and other game chants; even jokes that rely on rhythm, like knock-knock jokes.
- Collect visual rhythms with a digital camera: windows in rows, stairs, stacks of packages and boxes, trash cans lined up on the curb . . .

Play with Rhythm

- Turn a game of catch into a rhythm game by consciously varying the pace and placement of a bounced beach ball, tennis ball, or foam ball.
- The next time your child has a memorization task (for example, learning the multiplication tables), "warm up" with a rhythmic game using sound and movement.
- Clap out or use rattles to describe the rhythm of a weekday and the rhythm of a weekend day. Think about everyday rhythms like night/day, wake/sleep, work/play, etc. How are weekdays and weekend days different, the same?
- Read stories, poems, and songs that have definite rhythms. For young children, try Dr. Seuss books or *Chicka Chicka Boom Boom* by Bill Martin and John Archambault.
- Jump rope, learn to juggle, and play jacks.

Select, Create, and Make Rhythm

- Look for music that matches tasks you and your child can do together (a march, '50s rock 'n' roll, gospel, klezmer, opera, swing). Talk about whether a certain kind of musical rhythm makes the job easier or more fun.

- Next time you ask your child to do something, use a different spoken rhythm than the one you usually use for such requests. (Try drawling, speaking like an auctioneer, giving your words an up-and-down lilt, etc.)
- Time a task, such as making the bed, brushing teeth, or getting ready for school. Ask your child to try to do the task faster and faster every day, while timing the results with a stop watch. Talk about and notice which rhythms help or hinder the accomplishment of the task.
- Make a family calendar with repeating events and activities noted visually. Help your child understand the rhythms of the week. Keep a calendar of weather, moon phases or other natural events, as well as repeating events in your family life: grocery store visits, family outings, books read, hours of TV watched. What rhythms and cycles do you discover?
- Invent a family rhythm band. Make drums, rattles, and shakers with recyclable materials.

Rhythm

Rhythm at the Zoo

Collect Rhythm
- Look at animals (and the environment) for visual patterns and rhythms: dots, stripes, zigzags, grids, waves, spirals.
- Listen to animal sounds. Can you hear and repeat any rhythms in bird songs, animal calls, croaks, whistles, and squeaks?
- Watch and compare the rhythms of animals moving. Take photos or make sketches to record their rhythms.

Play with Rhythm
- Copy and clap out the rhythms of animal movements that you see. (Remember, people are animals, too.)
- Time your visit to coincide with feeding time. How does this change the rhythms you see?

Select, Create, and Make Rhythm
Back at home, use the ideas, rubbings, photos, and drawings you collected at the zoo for one or more of these rhythm projects:
- Make a rhythm painting of a day at the zoo on a big piece of paper.
- Depict as many animal rhythms as you can remember.
- As a family, play the rhythms of the zoo with your household rhythm band instruments. Take turns being the conductor and assigning the instruments and rhythms. Play the rhythms you collected or that you can imagine: the zoo waking up, the zoo in a thunder storm, the zoo at night.
- Play Saint-Saens "Carnival of the Animals," or another piece of music, and create your own dance of animal rhythms.

Rhythm at the Art Museum

Collect Rhythm
- Notice how different periods of art history have different rhythms. How are baroque paintings different in rhythm than Mexican folk art? Does the art from prehistoric times have a different rhythm from the art of medieval cathedrals?
- Using rhythm words, talk about the paintings you see and how the artist used rhythm to make the painting, sculpture, or other artwork more interesting to the eye.
- Can you find a painting that looks like jazz? Like a march? Like primitive drum beats? Like skipping down the sidewalk, or a bubble floating far above? Think of rhythm metaphors for the art you see.
- Some rhythm art to look for includes paintings by Mondrian, early American quilts, target paintings by Jasper Johns, pop art, and op art.

Play with Rhythm
- Translate the rhythms you see in a painting into a sound poem or a hand-clapped rhythm, and share with each other (quietly, if you are in a public gallery).

Select, Create, and Make Rhythm
- Back at home, using art books or postcard reproductions of some of the art you saw at the museum, make your own rhythm paintings or collages.
- Make a patchwork quilt from paper (or fabric if you are ambitious) inspired by rhythms collected at the museum or from art book investigations.

Rhythm

Special Rhythm Activity: Stickers, Stamps, and Prints _____
(Note: These activities are good for exploring shape as well.)

Collect Rhythm
- Put together a collection of commercially available stamps, such as the foam shape stamps sold in craft stores and online art stores. Select simple stamps that you can use with paint, large ink pads, or watercolor markers.
- Collect a variety of stickers in simple geometric and iconic shapes—dots, squares, triangles, stars, hearts, etc.
- Collect old kitchen utensils or other found objects that can be used as stamps: potato mashers, corks, cleaning tools, etc. Stamp your rhythm patterns in clay, in baker's clay (mixed from flour, salt, and water), with mud or sand, or on paper with paint.

Play with Rhythm
- Using your stamp and sticker collection, make rhythm pictures on a variety of kinds of paper.
- Try the "stamp" mode with different digital drawing programs, such as the Drawing Pad app or the Crazy Coloring Book app for Macs.

Select, Create, and Make Rhythm
- At the grocery store, purchase fruits and vegetables that, when cut in half, make interesting shapes: apples, celery, peppers, mushrooms. Using tempera paint or fabric craft acrylic, stamp patterns on paper or cloth. You can make family napkins, paper tablecloths for parties, or t-shirt designs with these rhythm experiments.
- Make a stamp or sticker pattern on long pieces of adding machine tape. Some patterns to try include favorite music, the rhythm of a day, the rhythm of a thunderstorm, a parade marching by, an argument, a party.
- Use found object stamps (such as metal potato mashers, spatulas, and wooden spools) with melted soy wax to make batik patterns. Find and follow instructions on the Internet for microwave soy wax batik and dyeing fabric. Use your fabric for curtains, dolls, quilts, or wall hangings. (Note: This is a hot-wax process that needs close adult supervision.)

Reflect _____
Of all the rhythm activities you tried, which ones were your child's favorites?
- Do you think your child has a special affinity for rhythm materials and projects?
- How does your sense of rhythm match or not match that of your child?
- Where and how and when in your family's everyday life could attention to rhythm make a difference in the quality of time you spend together?

This is my

Working Rhythm
Charlie

Rhythm: Field Notes

Write | Paste | Draw

Space

Space

Space Words

tight,

expansive,

fluid, cosmic,

random, arc,

loose, stage,

stadium, arch,

atrium, planet,

negative,

positive,

platform,

plateau, up,

down, over,

under, around,

inner, outer,

sky, manmade,

landlocked,

understory,

roadway,

cathedral,

bridge, page,

canvas, room,

undefined,

crowded,

empty

Range _____

Space is . . . around us, between us, and in us and everything else.

Description _____

Space is what we fill and what fills us. It is what we swim in and arrange and compartmentalize. It can be galactic or teensy-weensy tiny. Space is all about size. Space is relative rather than absolute, defined by frames and borders, boundaries and dimensions. Big compared to something smaller. Little compared to something larger.

Individuals and cultures have invisible borders that define where personal space ends and public space begins. Space is an emptiness that can be filled with all the other elements: lines, sounds, shapes, rhythms, light, movement, and the rest. Space can be an empty canvas, a hallway, an interval, a stage, an arena, a silence, a city. Space can be found in a cup, closet, cave, crater, cubbyhole, canyon, crevasse, or other container. We create planes, rockets, and kites to move through space. We watch birds soar in space and spiders spin webs that span space.

Connections _____

- Astronauts traverse big spaces; astronomers, even bigger spaces—though not in person.
- Choreographers and stage directors fill space with movement, story, and sound.
- Painters create illusions of space, exploring figure and ground, dimension and perspective, all upon a flat canvas.
- Graphic designers and web designers work with virtual layers in digital space.
- Potters pay as much attention to the inside as they do to the outside.
- Spelunkers explore inner space; so do doctors and medical researchers.
- Interior designers and decorators make spaces beautiful, exciting, functional, and dramatic.
- Architects are always thinking about space.
- Musicians fill silence (empty space) with sounds and rhythms.
- Type and font designers consider the spaces in and around letters, words, and paragraphs.
- Mathematicians define space in numbers and formulas, discovering the mysteries of abstract dimensions that we can think about but not see.

The Key Question _____

How do you like to fill space?

Looking for Space _____

Materials and Objects for Exploring and Playing with Space

- empty boxes
- blocks, including interesting shapes such as arches, cones, and triangular pieces
- other building toys, such as Legos, Lincoln Logs, geodesic sets
- straws and playdough for building models
- cards for building card houses
- cloth to create clothes and costumes that make a space for a body
- blankets and quilts to use for tents and tunnels
- an empty space
- containers for filling with different categories of things
- time
- a tree to climb
- the night sky and a star guide
- maps and globes
- blank paper and things to fill it with
- origami paper and instructions
- Planetary, the music catalog/playback tablet app and Star Walk, an app for star watching

Space

Talking about Space

The space within becomes the reality of the building.
—Frank Lloyd Wright

That great Cathedral space which was childhood.
—Virginia Woolf

To me every hour of the light and dark is a miracle. Every cubic inch of space is a miracle.   *—Walt Whitman*

Space is to place as eternity is to time.   *—Joseph Joubert*

Music was my refuge. I could crawl into the space between the notes and curl my back to loneliness.
—Maya Angelou

Space is big. You just won't believe how vastly, hugely, mind-bogglingly big it is. I mean, you may think it's a long way down the road to the drug store, but that's just peanuts to space.   *—Douglas Adams*

Darkness is to space what silence is to sound, i.e., the interval.
—Marshall McLuhan

What art offers is space—a certain breathing room for the spirit.   *—John Updike*

Space and light and order. Those are the things that men need just as much as they need bread or a place to sleep.
—Le Corbusier

Space at Home and In Your Neighborhood

Collect Space

- Collect spaces with a digital camera. Some categories to collect include tiny spaces, spaces inside of other spaces, doors and windows, and arches. Look for things hanging in space. Find different ways to "cut" the space.
- Take a walk around the block, and notice all the interesting hiding spaces you can spot along your route. In your home, find the best hiding spaces. Find your favorite-sized space.
- Make a collection of empty boxes to use for building, stacking, sorting, and knocking down.

Play with Space

- Create experiments to explore how air takes up space: blow up balloons and twist them into different spaces for air. Place a tissue inside a cup of water, then try to dunk it in water without wetting the tissue. Put a card over the top of a glass of water, turn the glass over, and remove your hand. What happens? Pour water into different shaped containers, experimenting with how much fits—can you guess?
- Fly a kite.
- Build cities, towns, and houses with blocks and building toys of different kinds. What kinds of materials work best for what kinds of spaces?

Select, Create, and Make Space

- Arrange a space in your home a new way. Rearrange your working or play spaces to be more organized, more functional, or more fun.
- Create paper airplanes, helicopters, and balloon rockets with paper, cardboard, and other recycled materials. What shapes fly through space the best? What goes farthest or highest or smoothest through the space of air?
- Build a dollhouse or other miniature model structure. Make your own furnishings for the spaces you build. Even a shoebox can become a tiny dollhouse room.
- Design and build a treehouse or playhouse.
- Invent the best possible storage and organizing system for your sense of space. Should you use open-topped boxes? Keep everything visible? Or everything hidden? Stacked? Cubbies? Locked treasure boxes? Bins? Sacks and bags?

Space

Space at the Zoo

Collect Space

- Notice the different kinds of enclosures for the different animals. Try to figure out why the zoo designers gave a particular animal the kind of space it has. Does your zoo use space well?
- Count how many different kinds of animal spaces you can find.
- Take photos of different animal spaces and videos of how animals use the spaces. What about the people spaces at the zoo?
- How do different groups of animals use space? Do they crowd together or stay far apart from each other? What about people at the zoo—can you tell who is a family by how closely they stay together? Notice spaces between and around animals and people.

Play with Space

- Observe animals with binoculars to bring their spaces closer to view.
- Use lookers (cardboard tubes or cards with square "looking holes" cut in them) to watch animals and parts of animals.

Select, Create, and Make Space

Back at home, use the ideas, photos, and drawings you collected at the zoo for one or more of these shape projects:

- Using a shoebox or other cardboard box, build a model diorama of an animal in its environment. Research the animal's home in its native territory. Compare what you learn to the zoo spaces you saw.
- Draw or paint a really big animal on butcher paper or on cut-open paper bags taped together, and also draw a tiny version on an index card. Which do you like best?

Space at the Art Museum

Collect Space

- Visit a sculpture gallery or garden, and notice how artists use 3-D space.
- How many different kinds of spaces does your art museum have? Do the spaces help to make the art more interesting? More beautiful? More dramatic?
- Look for the empty or negative space in sculptures and paintings. Most artists try to make the space *around* their objects as interesting as the space the objects use.

Play with Space

- Freeze your body to fit into the space of a figure or object in a painting.
- Act out a sculpture with movement, filling the space in the same manner as the sculpture.

Select, Create, and Make Space

- Back at home, play swinging statues. One person swings the second person around and lets go. The "swingee" freezes into a pose, making an interesting shape in space.

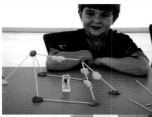

Space

Special Space Activity: An Adventure Playground in Your Backyard _____

(Note: You can adapt these activities to a playroom, a family room, or a child's bedroom.)

Collect Space

- Make a collection of materials that can be used for constructions that change and create space: blocks, boxes, chairs and sheets, logs and branches, sand, mud, clay, bricks, newspaper rolled into long thin building sticks, bamboo poles and mats, tents and tarps, junk and other stuff. Be sure to collect some old sheets and blankets.
- Look for ideas about building an adventure playground; search the Internet. Start with http://adventureplaygrounds.hampshire.edu/afternoon.html and http://popupadventureplay.org, two good sites. A pop-up playground, one that is temporary and can be easily assembled and disassembled, may be the practical choice for your home—or you may want to take on a more permanent project, including a constructed treehouse or play structure.
- Look around your house to determine the best place to build.

Play with Space

- First, play with the materials you have collected. How can they be combined? Attached? Stacked? Can you alter any of them by cutting or making holes in them?
- What objects or elements of the space you are in can be used in your adventure playground? A tree? A picnic table or lawn furniture? Sidewalks or grassy areas?

Select, Create, and Make Space

Construct your playground with the found materials you have collected. Some items may need adult help and supervision, but if you are building a "pop-up playground," most of the materials are easy to build using tape, staples, ropes, and wire. Try these ideas:

- Build a castle, fort, or walled kingdom.
- Construct a ship or boat "sailing" on the lawn, or a rocket ship to the stars.
- Lay out a maze, labyrinth, or obstacle course.
- Make a tent in which you can eat a meal or spend the night.

Reflect _____

- Of all the space activities you tried, which ones were your child's favorites?
- Do you think your child has a special affinity for spatial thinking and for organizing spaces?
- Does your child seem to prefer two-dimensional or three-dimensional spaces?
- Are boundaries, borders, and clearly-defined spaces important to your child?
- Could your child benefit from communications, routines, and daily structures that are spatially organized, such as making a special space for homework, another for play?
- How does your sense of space match or not match that of your child?
- Where and how and when in your family's everyday life could attention to space make a difference in the quality of time you spend together?

Space: Field Notes

Write | Paste | Draw

Movement

Movement

Movement Words

run, gallop,

slink, slither,

kick, stick,

lunge, loop,

zip, zoom,

clench, tackle,

leap, dance,

slump, stretch,

gesture, rip,

grimace,

evaporate,

condense,

retreat, retire,

race, shuffle,

slide, swing,

swim, stitch,

stir, dig, dip,

jump, dangle,

twitch, turn,

tug, tether,

twist, spiral,

spin, cast,

catch, waltz,

tango, polka,

poke, pry,

punch, float,

fling, reach,

stir, slice, slop,

slip, skip, hop

Range

Movement happens within and without our bodies, in nature, big and little. Movement happens in space and with its own rhythm.

Description

Movement is an action, a motion, a change of position. Movement takes us from here to there, from up to down, from forward to backward, to the left, to the right, and everywhere in between. We can see the effects of movement in the wind, water, cars, animals, human beings, gravity, and forces of all kind. We feel movement in the changes in our own muscles, breath, nerves, and bones, as well as when we gesture, express, respond, and go through space. We move as we travel, play, dance, work, and rearrange ourselves moment by moment.

We cannot see it, but we know that movement goes on continuously within—keeping our blood flowing, sending signals to and from our brains, and keeping all our functions functioning. We can sense movement in music and sound, and in our emotional responses. We can participate in movements such as marches, progressions, transactions, trends, and campaigns. We can use movement to choreograph people and ideas, to process ideas and information, and to make transitions from A to B. Even stillness has within it the movement of watching, breathing, and listening.

Connections

- A dancer uses his body to create movement ideas; so does a baseball player.
- A biologist can study the movement of muscles, cells, hormones, systems, and neurons.
- An acrobat studies stillness, balance, and movement by himself and with others.
- Every athlete is concerned with moving his muscles, with propelling herself through space and time, with finding the balance between control and risk.
- A mechanical engineer understands how machines and their parts move.
- Movement captured on film is the medium most important to a director.
- Business owners and commodity brokers understand the movement of goods, services, money, and investments.
- Movement is an important element of stories, films, theater, and performance. It literally moves the action along, communicating information about time, emotion, and interaction.
- People and animals move in amazing ways: up rock walls, across tightropes, through tunnels, in darkness, in very fast machines, underground, and in the air.
- Meteorologists study the movement of wind, water and air currents, and pressure zones.
- Bulldozers move earth. Trains move goods. Cranes move cables. Robots move automobiles along an assembly line. People learn to drive and control all these machines as they move.
- Earth makes big movements through space; the universe, even larger ones.
- Physicists study the big and little movements of forces seen and unseen.

The Key Question

What moves you? And what do you move?

Looking for Movement

Materials and Objects for Exploring and Playing with Movement
- your body
- jump ropes, balls, and wheeled toys
- bikes, trikes, and wagons
- ramps and trails
- sports fields and running tracks
- sidewalks (and roller skates)
- discarded machines (Note: Remove any electrical cords, fuses, or electronic components first.)
- wood, nails, and hammer
- dominoes to line up and knock down
- blocks for tower building

Movement

Talking about Movement

There is a vitality, a life-force, an energy, a quickening that is translated through you into action and because there is only one of you in all of time, this expression is unique. And if you block it, it will never exist through any other medium and be lost. —Martha Graham

Amazingly, the part of the brain that processes movement is the same part of the brain that's processing learning. —Eric Jenson

Sometimes you get a glimpse of a semicolon coming, a few lines farther on, and it is like climbing a steep path through woods and seeing a wooden bench just at a bend in the road ahead, a place where you can expect to sit for a moment, catching your breath. —Lewis Thomas

The dance is a poem of which each movement is a word. —Mata Hari

Give me a lever long enough and a fulcrum on which to place it, and I shall move the world. —Archimedes

The least movement is of importance to all nature. The entire ocean is affected by a pebble. —Blaise Pascal

My writing is like a ten-gallon spring. It can issue from the ground anywhere at all. On smooth ground it rushes swiftly on and covers a thousand li in a single day without difficulty. When it twists and turns among mountains and rocks, it fits its form to things it meets: unknowable. What can be known is, it always goes where it must go, always stops where it cannot help stopping—nothing else. More than that, even I cannot know. —Su Shih

- books for young children about movement: *From Head to Toe* by Eric Carle and *Jiggle Wiggle Prance* by Sally Noll
- digital toys and software apps such as TinkerBox, a game that teaches how to build simple and complex machines and movement puzzles; Wii dance and sports games; and so on

Movement at Home and In Your Neighborhood

Collect Movement
- Use a movie camera, the camcorder function on a phone, or a digital camera to record interesting movements. Some simple editing programs are easy enough for young children who have computer experience, or parents can help with the editing.
- Copy movements you see on a walk through the neighborhood: clouds, pets, people, tree branches.
- Visit a school track, sports field, gym, climbing wall, or another space where movement is paramount.
- Find the best places to run, climb, and make different movements—at home and in the community.
- Watch several different sports, dances, or people making things on television (or even better, in real life) and compare the movements and movement patterns.
- Read a newspaper sports page together and collect the movement words you find.
- Make a family collection of movement toys: different sizes of balls, jump ropes, hula hoops, juggling balls and scarves, large pieces of lightweight fabric (a parachute is the ultimate!), silk scarves, and bubble solution with bubble wands.

Play with Movement
- Teach your child classic movement games: tag, red rover, Mother may I, kickball, dodgeball, etc. For ideas and rules for more than 400 children's movement games from around the world, see http://www.fungameskidsplay.com/classicgames.htm
- How many ways can your child play with a ball, a silk scarf, a bottle of bubble solution?
- Pantomime people, animal, and machine movements you see.

Movement

Select, Create, and Make Movement
- Build an obstacle course with simple materials in your backyard or even indoors. Use boxes, ropes (on the ground to tiptoe along), and hula hoops.
- Invent your own kind of ball game. Make up the rules. Keep score.
- Build a set of ramps, roads, and other paths for wheeled cars or toys. Use blocks, boards, sheets of cardboard, boxes, and other simple recycled materials for tunnels, pathways, and gravity-directed movement.
- Put on favorite music and invent your own dances.
- Read stories and act out what happens.
- Practice over and over a movement you would like to do well: bouncing a ball, doing a backbend, balancing on one foot, using chopsticks, rotating a hula hoop, etc.

Movement at the Zoo

Collect Movement
- Watch how different animals move.
- Make videos to edit later.
- Capture movement with a still shot on your digital camera. Consider how blurs, zooms, and out-of-focus images can express movement.

Play with Movement
- With your own body, copy different kinds of animal movements you see—big cats, flying birds, excited monkeys, huge elephants, and so on.
- Take digital photos as you move the camera in different ways. Let the camera movement tell its own story.

Select, Create, and Make Movement
Back at home, use the ideas and photos and drawings you collected at the zoo for one or more of these movement projects:
- Invent an animal movement game (like charades), using as many real movements as you can remember.
- Tell a story about the animal movements you noticed.
- Edit your movement photos and videos into a slide show with transitions and moving special effects.
- Build an animal sculpture that moves. Find inspiration in the work of this street artist: Inflatable Bag Monsters: http://www.youtube.com/watch?v=PH6xCT2aTSo.

Movement at the Art Museum

Collect Movement
- Talk about the paintings you see with movement words: *fast, gentle, jazzy, sweeping, stagnant, still, windy, wave-filled.*
- Find examples of art that moves, such as mobiles by Alexander Calder. Look for movement captured in paintings: the movement of battle scenes and horse races, the movement of storms or fire, the movement of paint on a canvas.

Play with Movement
- Move your body to match or emphasize the movements you see in a painting or sculpture. Trace the movements you see with your finger, hand, or head.
- If a painting were to come to life, what would be the next movement?

Select, Create, and Make Movement
Back at home, use art books or postcard reproductions of some of the art you saw at the museum for one or more of the following movement projects:
- Make a moving sculpture, mobile, or pop-up book.
- Turn a piece of art into a story and act it out.

Movement

- Teach your child to use slideshow software that includes moving transitions between images. Use the photos you took at the museum to make your own moving slideshow.

Special Activity: Excursion to a Movement/Dance Performance

(Note: Substitute a sporting event if it suits your child better.)

Collect Movement
- Before the performance, find video clips or photos on websites about the performers or the dances being performed. Talk about the movement stories you will see and how dancers learn and practice their craft.
- Take along a sketchpad and draw some of the movements you see during the dance performance.
- Take photos, if this is allowed (but no flash!).

Play with Movement
- Follow the movements you see on stage with your eyes and imagination. How would you make those movements?
- What story is the movement telling you? During intermission and after the performance, talk about the stories and how movement told them. Were different kinds of stories being told?

Select, Create, and Make Movement
- What if you made your own version of the movement story you saw performed? What would you need to do and know?
- Move to different kinds of music. See how different styles of music change your movements.
- Make up your own movement story and perform it.
- Draw or paint a picture that captures the movements you saw in the performance.

Reflect

Of all the movement activities you tried, which ones were your child's favorites?
- Do you think your child has a special affinity for movement and kinesthetic learning?
- Does your child need to move in order to think? To move, in order to pay attention? To move physically through information, in order to learn?
- Could your child benefit from communications, routines, and daily structures that allow and encourage all kinds of movement?
- How does your sense of movement match or not match that of your child?
- Where and how and when in your family's everyday life could making time for movement make a difference in the quality of time you spend together?

Movement: Field Notes

Write | Paste | Draw

Texture

Texture

Texture Words

smooth,
scratchy,
glassy,
shiny,
cracked,
plaid,
polka dots,
ribbed,
wiry, dog's
ear, curly,
wavy, oily,
fuzzy, hairy,
silky, ashy,
prickly,
woven, wet,
woolly, slick,
melting,
layered,
soft, glossy,
doughy,
puffy,
bumpy,
touch,
slimy, cool,
chewy,
tender,
velvety

Range

Texture is everywhere at our fingertips (and at the range of our eyesight, too—both near and far). Consider the texture of a handful of sand and the texture of a hillside covered in trees.

Description

Whether it is actual (the way something feels to our touch) or apparent (how it looks to our eyes), texture adds dimension, pattern, and complexity to our world of senses. Textures can be smooth or rough, wet or dry, slick or bumpy, intricate or plain. Textures may be repeated patterns, like corn on a cob, reeds woven into a basket, cells in a beehive, or marbles in a glass jar. We see textures in cracked earth, a shiny car bumper, a page of text. Textures can be seen through the lens of a microscope or a telescope, or experienced with eyes closed tight. Sometimes textures define the unique material qualities of an object, such as glass, metal, fur, rubber, or silk.

We sense textures with our hands and skin but also with our mouth and ears. Bring to mind the texture (and taste) of sandy grit on a beach-eaten hotdog, the slimy feel of over-cooked asparagus…the frozen buttery silk of ice cream.

Polyphony or counterpoint is heard as aural texture—the interweaving of one or more lines of sound. Actors, writers, and film directors texture their creative work with nuance, undercurrents, and things seen but not talked about, adding layers of meaning that create texture within the work. We sense texture in networks, such as fishing nets, building trusses, and a web page. Texture defines quality and style as it enriches, relates to, or intertwines ideas, objects, creations, and sometimes, people.

Connections

- A weaver works with texture in patterns, forms, and mathematics.
- A geographer creates textured maps that distinguish physical characteristics of a place.
- A naturalist notices the interconnected textures that relate animals to one another—as in the kinds of nests they build or the hard, soft, or seedy things they eat—as well as the physical textures, such as their fur or feathers, that distinguish species.
- A singer finds ways to use the texture of sound as part of his or her vocal style.
- A hairdresser must master the skills to cut, color, and style different textures of hair.
- Doctors and nurses use texture information to diagnose disease and wellness, noticing the texture of skin, hair, muscle tone, mucus, sweat, and other secretions.
- Texture is always part of an artist's toolbox, whether in paint, clay, quilts, video, photography, or other media.

The Key Question

How is texture a messenger of connection, complexity, and interdependence? Or, how important is texture to you?

Looking for Texture

Materials and Objects for Exploring and Playing with Texture

- fabric, trim, and yarn
- recycled materials and packaging (bubble wrap, plastic, metal tops and lids, plastic foam)
- interior decor and architecture sample books
- potter's clay and/or playdough
- rubber and foam stamps
- stickers, such as coding dots and tiny shiny stars
- cardboard
- water and sand
- beans and other dry foods with interesting textures

Talking about Texture

Has anyone yet said publicly how nice it is to write on rubber with a ballpoint pen? The slow, fat, ink-rich line rolled over a surface at once dense and yielding, makes for a multidimensional experience no single sheet of paper can offer. —Nicolson Baker

How swiftly the strained honey of afternoon light flows into darkness. —Lisel Mueller

Some people weave burlap into the fabric of our lives and some weave gold thread. Both contribute to make the whole picture beautiful and unique. —Anonymous

Experience has taught me, when I am shaving of a morning, to keep watch over my thoughts, because, if a line of poetry strays into my memory, my skin bristles so that the razor ceases to act. The seat of this sensation is the pit of the stomach. —A.E. Housman

Moisture and color and odor thicken here. The hours of daylight gather atmosphere. —Robert Frost

The verbal poetical texture of Shakespeare is the greatest the world has known, and is immensely superior to the structure of his plays as plays. With Shakespeare it is the metaphor that is the thing, not the play. —Vladimir Nabokov

Indifference is isolation. In difference is texture and wonder. —Edwin Schlossberg

Texture at Home and In Your Neighborhood

Collect Texture

- Make a texture collection in your backyard or neighborhood, filling a grocery bag with found textures. A good place to look is on a short stroll down an alleyway, near a railroad right-of-way, or in a park. Children need to be careful, but they can find all kinds of textured "beautiful trash" during such a walk.
- Collect textures by making rubbings. Put a sheet of strong but thin paper over a textured surface. Use the side of a crayon or piece of chalk to make an impression of the textures you find.
- Collect texture photos with a digital camera.
- Take a "blind" walk with your eyes closed or covered, noticing textures of the walkway, the walls, the sounds around you.
- Look in your closet and drawers, and explore the clothing and other textures you find there.
- Talk about moods and behaviors in terms of texture: "Are you feeling itchy and scratchy? You can't seem to stop fidgeting. What would make you feel smooth and creamy?"

Play with Texture

- Make texture collages with decorator samples, cut paper, beautiful trash from your collections, recycled materials from the kitchen and office, and your surface rubbings.
- Play a texture guessing game: Put textured items in a sack, box, or bag. Let children reach inside and describe the textures they feel.
- Make a sand, mud, and water table outdoors for exploring texture. For a temporary version, fill several dishpans or large cookie sheets with different textures, up to an inch deep: sand, gravel, rice, beans, small pasta, mud, water. Play with them separately and mixed together.

- Make pressed, modeled, and shaped textures with packaged (thawed and ready to bake) or homemade bread dough. Let it rise and bake for textured breads. Or try the same with inedible baker's clay. Add 1 cup water to 1 cup salt and 3 cups flour, knead it well, and bake at 250 degrees Fahrenheit until hard.
- Explore textures in pottery clay (or air-dry modeling clay) by making textured tiles, cutting or rolling slab pieces about half an inch thick. Children can use dowels, wooden and metal kitchen utensils, metal forks, plastic knives, bottle caps, and other such tools to make various texture impressions.
- Play with textures of food while eating. What feels good in the mouth? Make an inventory.
- Garden together. Talk about the textures you notice in the plants, the earth, and even the weather.
- Listen to music together, and talk about what textures you hear. Is the music rough or smooth? Is it layered with sounds or woven together with different tunes? How many instruments do you hear, and what texture belongs to each one?

Select, Create, and Make Texture

- Have your texture tiles commercially fired (or use the air-dry clay) and let children select and assemble them into a texture mural for an outdoor or indoor artwork. Epoxy the tiles to a piece of plywood for durable display.
- Translate a piece of your child's art into a design for a quilt, wall hanging, doll, or pillow. Let your child select the texture fabrics to use. Iron-on bonding web makes this easy, but using a sewing machine to assemble the fabric pieces will make for a more durable piece of artwork.
- Create a book about the furry and feathery textures of all the animals in your neighborhood, using photos, drawings, and children's stories of the animals

Texture

they see. Use one of the "publish-on-demand" websites, such as Blurb, Lulu, or AdoramaPix for a professional-looking book.

Texture at the Zoo

Collect Texture
- Collect stray feathers in and around the aviary.
- Collect memories of the textures you experience as you touch the coats of animals at the petting zoo. Record the textures in sketches or photographs.
- Look for examples of how texture helps camouflage animals, insects, and birds.
- Look for textured patterns on animals and discuss what purpose the textures might serve.
- How many textures of hair, horns, and hooves can you collect?
- Zoos are often filled with exotic textured plants and foliage. See how many new textures of leaves and bark you can find.

Play with Texture
- When you carefully observe an animal, how many texture words can you use to describe the way it looks and behaves?
- Go on a scavenger hunt for a particular texture—rough, spotty, hairy, scaly, fuzzy, sleek—taking photos or making drawings of what you find.
- Take your rubbing kit (paper and oil pastels, chalk, or crayons) and record different surface textures: embossed signs, tree bark, grates, and more.
- What animal can you look like? Experiment with your hair to make different textures: braid, frizz, press, tease, tufts, etc. What animal can you look like?

Select, Create, and Make Texture
Back at home, use the ideas, rubbings, photos, and drawings you collected at the zoo for one or more of these texture projects:
- Make texture prints inspired by your zoo visit. On large paper, draw simple animal shapes (older kids can make their own; parents can help younger ones). Then use cut vegetable stamps or other paint stamps to make patterns and textures on the animals.
- Make up a skit or story about animal textures: "How the Alligator Got his Tough Skin" or "What Made the Elephant So Wrinkled?" Using fabric scraps, yarn, and paper scraps, make a texture collage of one or more of the animals you saw at the zoo. (For young children, parents can start by cutting out the simple shape of a favorite animal.) The collage might even become the pattern for a stitched and sewn doll or a wall hanging.

Texture at the Art Museum

Collect Texture
- Use the art museum as a site for a texture scavenger hunt using a digital camera or sketchbook to capture the textures you see.
- Using texture words, talk about the art you see and how the artist used texture to make the painting, sculpture, or other artwork more interesting to the eye.
- Notice and talk about the textures of different art media: bronze versus glass, oil paint versus pastel, ink versus watercolor, carved wood versus clay.
- Look for opposites: hard/soft, wet/dry, smooth/bumpy, gritty/silky.
- Look for artwork created with fiber, fabric, yarn, string, or wire.

Play with Texture
- Translate the textures you see in a painting into a sound poem and share with each other (quietly, if you are in a public gallery).
- If the museum has a teaching gallery or children's area, explore the textures that you are allowed to touch in the special gallery. Some museums provide

opportunities for families to experience art work and materials in "please touch" areas.

- Imagine you are touching a particular piece of work. Blow up the movement of that tactile experience and share it with each other. How could you move your hand with the swooshy feeling of a brush stroke through oil paint or the carved smooth texture of a marble sculpture?

Select, Create, and Make Texture
Back at home:
- Use a postcard of a piece of art that you saw to inspire a texture collage with your collection of recycled materials, fabric, yarn, etc.
- Learn to weave, crochet, knit, or quilt.
- Use different drawing and painting materials to explore, compare, and contrast the textural quality of different media. Try as many of these as possible: charcoal, pastel, watercolor, oil paint, acrylic, tempera paint. Use a variety of different sizes, textures, and kinds of brushes to explore different textures on paper. Paint on a variety of kinds of paper and surfaces: board, canvas, watercolor paper, handmade paper, tissue paper, plastic film. Then use your favorite kind of paints, brushes, and painting surface to make a piece of art for your home.

Special Activity for Texture: Build a Texture Tunnel _____
This can be an ongoing project that takes several work/play sessions to complete. It's a fun activity for a child's birthday party or a sleepover.
1. Make a collection of recyclable textures and your child's texture collages. Collect old blankets, rugs, scraps of fabric, packing materials, discarded clothing, and other interesting textures.
2. Assemble four or five large cardboard cartons (large enough for your child to crawl through, such as appliance boxes). Open up two ends and tape the cartons together with packaging tape to make a tunnel. Reinforce as needed by propping the boxes up with chairs or against the wall.
3. Explore painted visual textures on the outside of the boxes by painting textures and texture patterns with different tools and brushes.
4. Cut windows and peep holes in the sides of the texture tunnel.
5. Fill the inside surfaces of the tunnel boxes with attached or rearrangeable textures: scraps of fabric, rug, packing materials, pillows, cotton, yarn, string and yarn webs, bubble wrap, etc. Some textures can be wired or tied to the "walls" and "floor" of the tunnel using string or flexible pipe cleaners. (Note: Parents can use a hot-glue gun and glue to adhere tricky surfaces, but be sure to keep little fingers away.)
6. Crawl through and play in the finished texture tunnel. If you wish, each box can explore a different category of texture: earth textures, sky texture, water textures, or rough textures, slick textures, and stringy textures.

Reflect _____
- Of all the texture activities you tried, which ones were your child's favorites?
- Did any of these texture activities strike a chord with your child or spark an "aha" moment?
- Do you think your child has a special affinity for texture and tactile learning?
- Does your child need to use his or her hands in order to feel involved and engaged?
- Could your child benefit from communications, routines, and daily structures that allow for and encourage tactile and manual interactions and activities?
- How does your sense of texture match or not match that of your child?
- Where and how and when in your family's everyday life could involving your child with hands-on interaction and activity make a difference?

Texture: Field Notes

Write | Paste | Draw

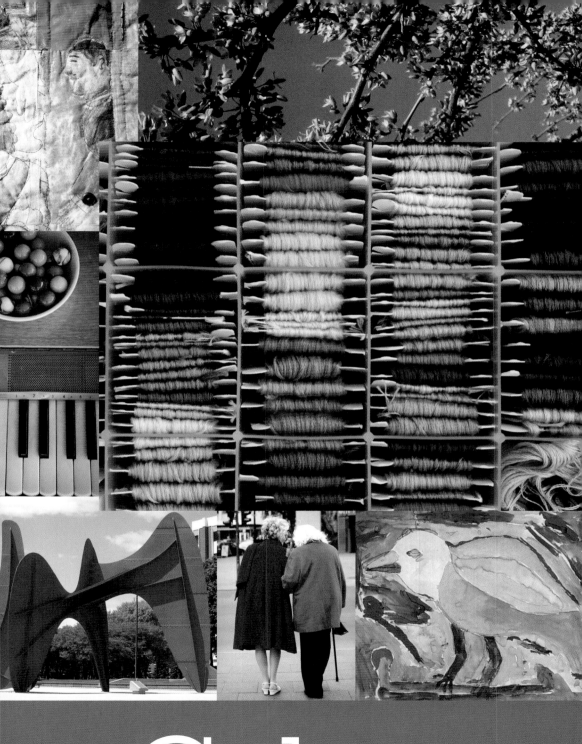

Color

Color

Range

One of the most visible and notable elements, color can be bold or subtle, and ever-changing in both the man-made and natural environment. In the mind and body, color evokes emotion, meaning, and conscious and unconscious behaviors.

Description

Color gives us the world of emotions, intensity, and hue. Color is seen but also sensed though other sensory channels—it can inspire or soothe or excite both our eyes and our emotions. Each world culture has developed its own language of color and has assigned emotional meaning and import.

Color helps us connect and separate the objects in our world. Color defines the seasons and other patterns in our lives. We can get a sense of color from the language of a poem, the timbre of a musical instrument or a voice, the taste of a spice, the commentary of a sportscaster. We use color to enhance our homes, our gardens, our cities, ourselves. We connect to the colors of our flag, our team, our skin, our traditions, our heritage. We play one color against another in fashion, in sports, in art, in war.

Color has a science, too, with its own lexicon, rules, and physical activity in the eye and the brain. When our eyes are saturated with one color, they long for its complement. Hues, tones, tints, and shades give color an infinite range—mixing color pigments and colored lights result in different artistic, chemical, and physical effects. Color plays tricks on us, since we see color only in contrast to the other colors around it.

Connections

- A painter creates impact, design, and emotion with color.
- A gardener designs living, seasonally changing patterns with colorful blossoms and foliage.
- A naturalist understands divergent species though color distinctions in plants and animals, an astronomer in planets and stars.
- A chef puts color on the plate and before the eye with just as much intent as he or she uses taste.
- Every sportscast has its color commentary, to add interest and human emotion to the game.
- Marketers pay close attention to color trends and color crazes.
- Psychologists study how color affects behaviors as we dine, sleep, study, and buy.

The Key Question

How do different colors evoke different behaviors and emotions?

Looking for Color

Materials and Objects for Exploring and Playing with Color

- water tinted with food coloring
- paint
- shaving foam with food dyes or concentrated liquid watercolor
- Jell-O and molds such as ice cube trays plastic containers filled with ice, juice, or blended fruit
- leaves and flowers
- animals and people
- painting to music
- colored cellophane or eyeglasses
- digital camera
- *Frederick, Little Blue and Little Yellow,* and other books by Leo Lionni
- *Rooster's Off to See the World* by Eric Carle
- *The Night the Moon Fell* or *The Race of Toad and Deer* by Pat Mora
- paint programs using phone or tablet apps such as "Drawing Pad" (www.drawingpadapp.com)
- color hue test: http://www.colormunki.com/game/huetest_kiosk
- color mixing: http://itunes.apple.com/us/app/colormixxa/id375018245?mt=8

Color

Talking about Color

The Mediterranean has the color of mackerel—change-able I mean. You don't always know if it is green or violet, you can't even say it's blue, because the next moment the changing reflection has taken on a tint of rose or gray. —Vincent van Gogh

White . . . is not a mere absence of colour; it is a shining and affirmative thing, as fierce as red, as definite as black. —G. K. Chesterton

Color is the place where our brain and the universe meet. —Paul Klee

I found I could say things with color and shapes that I couldn't say any other way—things I had no words for. —Georgia O'Keeffe

The sound of colors is so definite that it would be hard to find anyone who would express bright yellow with bass notes or dark lake with treble. —Wassily Kandinsky

If one says, "Red" (the name of a color), and there are fifty people listening, it can be expected that there will be fifty reds in their minds. And one can be sure that all these reds will be very different. —Josef Albers

Color at Home and In Your Neighborhood

Collect Color
- Make a set of colored "lookers." Tape colored plastic or cellophane over the end of a cardboard tube or over the lenses of some discarded eyeglass frames. Look though the colors to see how the world appears when every-thing is tinted with red, blue, or yellow. Also, for 3-D effects, try putting different colors up to each eye.
- Look at the colors in your room. Find the same colors in pieces of paper or magazine photos. Do the same with your closet of clothing. What colors do you like? Do they show up in your clothes and space? Is color important to you?
- Start a color collection scrapbook, divided into color families. Add photos, scraps of fabric, postcards, maga-zine pictures, wrapping paper, and package papers, etc.
- Visit a garden or nursery for color inspiration. Also look at *Planting a Rainbow* by Lois Ehlert.

Play with Color
- Paint or draw with pastels while listening to a favorite piece of classical music. Don't worry about making it look like anything special; just play with the colors that come to mind.
- Mix food dyes or saturated liquid watercolors with a small blob of (unscented) shaving foam. Start with the primary hues and let children see how many other colors they can make.
- Finger paint with colored shaving foam, with various paints, with mud, or with different colors of pudding.
- Assemble a collection of colored papers for cutting and pasting. See how one color looks against different background colors. What colors play games with your eyes? Experiment with afterimages: Stare at one bright color for a minute, then look at a white sheet of paper. What color do you see, and what is its relationship to the color you stared at?
- Take a "color walk" in your neighborhood with a digi-tal camera. Collect photographs of colors you notice.

You might want to focus on one family of colors: reds, blues, greens, etc. Edit your photos and make a slide show to share with family members.

Select, Create, and Make Color
- Make a color wall with your child by taping or pinning a collection of colors to one wall in his or her room. Let your child plan and select the color for new room purchases or paint, when appropriate. Paint at least one wall your child's favorite color, and let your child help. If you can't paint, hang a large, stretched panel of colored fabric, as if it were a painting.
- Tie-dye an all-cotton shirt (use the newer dyes and tie-dye paints found in the craft store for no-bleed success). Look for pattern ideas on the Internet—for example, at http://www.kinderart.com/textiles/easytiedye.shtml.
- Invent a color-coded organizational system and room map with your child, assigning specific colors to toys and other possessions, matched to their storage spaces. Turn cleanup time into a color-matching game.
- Dismantle an inexpensive kaleidoscope and then invent a new one with better, more colorful parts. Carefully remove the end lens on the part that spins, replace the little other parts inside with other items such as colored beads, tiny foil stars, bits of cellophane, etc.

Color

Color at the Zoo

Collect Color

- Pick a particular color or kind of color pattern or animal part (for example beaks, spots, or feathers) to collect using a digital camera or sketchbook. How many colors of animal eyes can you find? The aviary and reptile houses at zoos are very good hunting grounds for color.
- Talk about camouflage and how animals and insects and birds are often colored to blend into (or stand out from) their environment. Look for examples to collect. Imagine what kind of natural world the animals must live in when they are in the wild.
- What color symbols or icons does the zoo use to tell you about the animals, about where to go, and about different areas and activities?

Play with Color

- Plan a color-coded family (or group) outfit to wear to the zoo, using color to define your "tribe."
- When you stop to look closely at an animal, see how many colorful words you can use to describe the way it looks and behaves.
- Go on a color scavenger hunt at the zoo, taking photos or making drawings of what you find.
- Paint your child's face with colored face paint or makeup to look like his or her favorite animal.
- Notice how different species of the same family of animals (reptiles, big cats, bears) are distinguished by color as one defining factor.
- Make a list of the ten most colorful animals you see on your visit to the zoo. (For a great list, see this from BBC Earth at http://listverse.com/2010/09/21/top-10-colorful-animals/.)

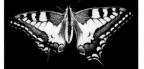

Select, Create, and Make Color

Back at home, use the ideas and photos and drawings you collected at the zoo for one or more of these color projects:

- Make an animal mask or costume, being true to the colors of the animal. Or imagine what the animal might look like if its native environment were some-place different. What would a lion look like if it lived on an iceberg? What kind of camouflage stripes would a tiger have who lived at the supermarket? What colors would a parrot's feathers be if it wanted to blend in to the jungle instead of standing out?
- Make up a skit, short play, or storybook about the animal colors: "How the Panda Bear became Black and White" or "What Made the Flamingo Pink?"
- Paint pictures of the animals you saw at the zoo, changing their colors and color patterns to blend in with a world of your imagination.

Color at the Art Museum

Collect Color

- Go on a color scavenger hunt at the art museum using a digital camera or, if allowed, colored pencils. Use your tools to collect colored shapes and/or textures. Pick one color or family of colors to focus on, seeking it throughout time and art history.
- Using color words, talk about the paintings you see and how the colors make you feel: *restful, excited, energetic, sleepy, busy, worried, angry.*

Play with Color

- Tell a color story while standing in front of a painting or other work of art. Use color words and emotions to describe what you see.
- Take your color collection scrapbook with you (or even a set of color paint chips from the home and garden store). Match the colors you see with the

colors you find in the museum. Back at home, make your own paintings, using the same colors.

Select, Create, and Make Color
Back at home:
- Using art books or postcard reproductions of some of the art you saw at the museum, make a colorful mural, painting on canvas, or quilt collage.
- After looking at a book or the work of a famous artist, try painting in the artist's style. Even young children can be inspired by a great artist's work!
- Explore the work of glass artist Dale Chihuly, even if only online (www.chihuly.com). Visit a glass-blowing studio in your own community.

Special Activity: Color in the Supermarket and the Kitchen

Collect Color
- In the kitchen, make a collection of objects and/or fruits and vegetables, and sort them by color and hue. Can you make a rainbow arrangement? Or categorize them into color "families?"
- At the supermarket, talk to your child about the colors you see. What new names can you invent for the colors (for example, eggplant purple, pinto brown)?
- Notice what colors are popular for marketing different kinds of products. Are soap packages the same color as soup cans?

Play with Color
- Layer three different colors of Jell-O to make rainbow parfaits.
- Dye eggs, even if it's not Easter.
- Tint juice and other beverages with food colorings. How cool is it to drink blue milk?

Select, Create, and Make Color
- Plan a menu with your child that is mostly one color (red, green, yellow), using simple recipes and preparations that your child can help with. Select plates, table decor, and other appropriate props for a color celebration meal.
- Make "jigglers," using gelatin in several flavors and colors made with 1/4 cup less water than called for. Let it set in a sheet pan, then cut with cookie cutters into colorful shapes.
- Purchase a rainbow of ordinary and unusual vegetables that can be used in a salad. Make the most colorful salad you can and see how it tastes. Do the same with fruits.
- What can you do in your dining room to make meals more restful, peaceful, or more appetizing? Can you and your child design colorful table linens, chair pillows, or wall decor with colors that make mealtimes happy and harmonious?

Reflect
- Of all the color activities you tried, which ones were your child's favorites?
- Did any of these color activities strike a chord with your child or spark an "aha" moment?
- Do you think your child has a special affinity for color?
- Is your child sensitive emotionally to the colors that surround him or her?
- Could your child benefit from communications, routines, and daily structures that use color to code, sort, signal, or emphasize information? Could reading and retention be aided by the use of colored highlighter pens?
- How does your sense of color match or not match that of your child?
- Where and how and when in your family's everyday life could using color consciously or using color the way an artist uses color make a difference?

Color: Field Notes

Write | Paste | Draw

Shape

Shape

Shape Words

round, square,

sinuous,

voluptuous,

angular,

freeform,

triangular,

inflated,

deflated,

polygon, sphere,

cone, silhouette,

distinct,

pompous,

geometric,

regular, irregular,

large, tiny,

heart-shaped,

narrow, solid,

hollow, cube,

octagonal,

ovoid, ball,

asymmetrical,

bulbous,

node, circle,

blob, ornate,

squashed,

irregular,

rectangular,

concave,

convex, rigid

Range

Shape is found easily in the man-made and natural environments. In the mind, a shape can be the outline or the essence of a piece of writing, design, or possibility.

Description

Shape can be seen, touched, and understood as an invisible element. With all its dimensions at its disposal, shape (whether 3-D or 2-D) separates insides from outsides. Shape creates a unity, an identity, a gestalt.

We spot shapes from a distance or up close in a microscope. We see shapes all around us. People, animals, vegetables, bottles, shadows, clouds, dwellings, automobiles, shoes, blocks, bones, liquid storage tanks, and planets all have distinctive shapes by which they can be identified. Silhouettes can be recognized without any other sensory information, and shape icons often tell us everything we need to know.

We touch shapes and create tactile shapes. Shirts, shoes, handles, pedals, chairs, knobs, ear buds, keyboards, and other shapes are designed to fit our human shapes. We shape reed, clay, wood, metal, plastic, dough, and many other raw materials through our hands-on work.

We can sense the shape of ideas, thoughts, plans, and schemes. We know when something is in "good shape" or when it needs to "be knocked into shape" or "shaped up." Shapes help us define an object, concept, or future, and to differentiate one from another. Something is or is not part of one shape or another. Shape is definite, although it can morph and change from one to another.

Connections

- A potter makes shapes of pots, platters, cups, and saucers.
- A landscaper knows how to use the shapes of trees, plants, and foliage to create a natural space with a specific feel, quality, and style.
- A naturalist identifies animals, plants, fossils, and other living and nonliving life using shape information.
- Designers create new shapes for clothes, furniture, cars, toys, and many, many other things.
- A chemist or physicist understands which molecules are which by understanding the shape arrangements of the atomic elements.
- Teachers "shape" learning experiences and lesson plans for others.
- Dancers use their bodies to make specific kinds of shapes as they move.
- Musicians talk about the shape of sounds, and different instruments create different kinds of sounds determined in part by the shape of the instrument.

The Key Question

Why do things have the shapes they do?

Looking for Shape

Materials and Objects for Exploring and Playing with Shape

- potter's clay
- playdough or bread dough
- mud and naturally occurring clay in stream beds
- cookie cutters and rolled-out dough
- molds for gelatin, such as ice cube trays or plastic containers filled with ice, juice, or blended fruit
- rocks and stones
- animals and people
- shadows
- stencils and stamps
- torn and cut paper (snowflakes, *papel picado* flags, etc.)
- jigsaw puzzles, both "real" and digital (Shape-O ABC's is a fun puzzle app for the iPad.)
- simple vector drawing programs on the computer
- digital camera

Shape

Talking about Shape

The sky is round, and . . . the earth is round like a ball, and so are all the stars. The wind, in its greatest power, whirls. Birds make their nests in circles, for theirs is the same religion as ours. The sun comes forth and goes down again in a circle. The moon does the same and both are round. Even the seasons form a great circle in their changing, and always come back to where they were. The life of a man is a circle from childhood to childhood, and so it is in everything where power moves. —Black Elk

The square is not a subconscious form. It is the creation of intuitive reason. It is the face of the new art. The square is a living, royal infant. It is the first step of pure creation in art. Before it, there were naïve deformities and copies of nature. Our world of art has become new, nonobjective, pure. —Kasimir Malevich

We shape our tools and afterwards our tools shape us. —Marshall McLuhan

Philosophy is written in this grand book—I mean the universe—which stands continually open to our gaze, but it cannot be understood unless one first learns to comprehend the language and interpret the characters in which it is written. It is written in the language of mathematics, and its characters are triangles, circles, and other geometrical figures, without which it is humanly impossible to understand a single word of it. —Galileo Galilei

Form follows function—that has been misunderstood. Form and function should be one, joined in a spiritual union. —Frank Lloyd Wright

I said to myself, I have things in my head that are not like what anyone has taught me—shapes and ideas so near to me—so natural to my way of being and thinking that it hasn't occurred to me to put them down. I decided to start anew, to strip away what I had been taught. —Georgia O'Keeffe

Shape at Home and In Your Neighborhood

Collect Shape

- Cut shaped holes (not just circles, squares, and triangles—make unusual shapes) in the middle of index cards or pieces of cardboard, leaving the card intact. Look through the shaped holes to find the same or similar shapes in and around your home. Record your collection by drawing, tearing, or cutting paper, or take photos of them and make a slide show or album on your computer.
- Look at the shapes of mugs, glasses, and cups in your kitchen cupboards. Make a "museum of shapes" on the table. To explore these shapes further, you can fill several of these different shapes with gelatin liquid (such as Jell-O), refrigerate to set, then unmold to see what the inside shape is like.
- Take photos of all the various types of leaves you can find in your neighborhood. See how many different leaf shapes you can collect. Identify the names of the trees from the leaf shape photos. The camera phone or tablet app Leafsnap (from the University of Maryland, Columbia University, and the Smithsonian Institution) can help.
- How many different shapes of leaves can one kind of tree have? Look carefully for the little differences in shapes.
- Take it further: Press your leaf collection in a discarded telephone book or other heavy volume (waxed paper can be used to protect the pages). When the leaves have dried, use them for other projects. (Look at *Leaf Man* by Lois Ehlert for an idea of how to write a story with leaf shapes.)

- Take a "shape walk" in your neighborhood. Using a digital camera or drawing in a sketchbook, collect shapes you like. Or, you might want to just collect one kind of shape: circles, triangles, squares, irregular, etc. Edit your photos and make a slide show or art exhibit of your sketches to share with family members.
- Look at shapes of fruits and vegetables in the supermarket. Use *Growing Vegetable Soup* by Lois Ehlert for inspiration.

Play with Shape

- Using markers, oil pastels, or crayons, trace the shapes of objects you find in and around your home. Instead of using purchased stencils, find objects, set them on plain paper, and carefully draw around the shapes.
- Use a photo program or drawing program (such as the "stamp" filter in Photoshop or Silhouetter, the camera phone app) to translate photographs your child takes into shape images and silhouettes. Print or use for a slide show.
- Sew a tube of stretch knit fabric large enough for your child to climb into and explore the shapes his or her body can make, pushing and pulling on the fabric. Take photos so your child can see the shapes.
- Use a copier to make a booklet of simple shapes drawn by your child (circles, squares, or triangles for youngest kids; more complex shapes for older ones). Then, finish each shape by completing it as a drawing of a different object or scene.
- Play with tangrams, the ancient Chinese shape puzzles, that use seven different shapes to match a challenge picture. You can purchase or make a cardboard, wood, or

Shape

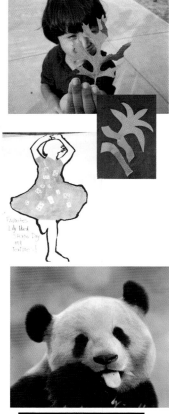

plastic tangram set, or find many versions online or as phone apps. (Tangram XL Free is one).
- Make cutout cookies (or try a virtual cookie-making game like the Cookie Doodle app) and experiment with different tools for making cookie shapes.

Select, Create, and Make Shape
- Make a "me paper" by tracing the shape of your child in different poses on a large piece of butcher paper or on cut-open paper bags taped together. Trace with pencil, and then (for extra impact) paint around the child's shape with black paint or a thick marker. Your child can fill his or her body shape with a shape collection or other collections of Sensory Alphabet favorites.
- Imagine, storyboard, and make a simple animation using camera shots of moving shapes with your child. Set up a tripod to make this easier, keeping the camera in the same place above a tabletop "stage." Shoot a few frames of video, or one slide, of each "scene," moving the shapes around on the stage to tell a story. Add music with a simple music program if you can, matching the shapes to sounds that fit. Make a low-tech animation by drawing a shape on every page of a small book of "sticky notes." Flip the pages to see the shapes "morph" and move.

Shape at the Zoo

Collect Shape
- Pick a particular animal part, and using a camera or paper and pencil, collect shapes belonging to this category. For example, make a collection of animal feet, ears, or noses. Use shape words to describe what you see and notice. Compare and contrast the shapes of all the noses of different animals. Why do you think the noses are shaped the way they are? What would each particular nose be good for? (Also look at books like *What Do You Do With a Tail Like This?* by Steve Jenkins and Robin Page.)
- Notice how your zoo is organized. Does the zoo have a certain shape to it? Are all the mammals together? Or are all the animals from Africa grouped together? What kinds of organizational shapes do you notice?
- What shape symbols or icons does the zoo use to tell you about the animals, about where to go, and about different areas and activities?
- At the zoo, decide which animal right now is the most interesting to you. Spend a bit more time with that animal, noticing as much as you can about it, especially about the shapes you see in the animal—maybe shapes of spots, shapes of body parts, shapes of its home and environment, shapes it makes in moving. Collect the shapes of this animal with photos, drawings, and in your mind's eye.

Play with Shape
- Take turns making your body into the shapes of the animals you see. Share your best animal shapes.
- Draw the shapes of animal noses (or other body parts) in the air, using your hand and arm.
- Make clay animals with modeling clay or playdough.
- Learn to make animal shadows with your hands and fingers.
- Eat animal crackers, finding the right cookie shape to eat at each enclosure. Are the shapes correct?

Select, Create, and Make Shape
Back at home, use the ideas, photos, and drawings you collected at the zoo for one or more of these shape projects:
- Make animal cut-out cookies using cookie cutters of the animals you saw.

Shape

- Make a book of the animal body part that you collected, for example, *The Book of Noses.* Use photos, drawings, or paper cutouts. If you wish, transform favorite shapes into silhouettes with a drawing or photo software program. (Also look at *Oodles of Animals* by Lois Ehlert for inspiration.)
- Make up a skit, short play, or storybook about the animal shapes you collected: "How the Elephant got his Trunk and the Bear His Big Nose."
- Paint your hands and fingers to look like different animals. (See the book *Hanimals* by Mario Mariotti for ideas and examples.)
- Make an animal fruit parade, using cut and whole fruit, raisins, toothpicks, parsley, and other edibles. Eat your parade for lunch. (See the book *Play with Your Food* by Joost Elffers for ideas.)

Shape at the Art Musuem _____

Collect Shape
- Choose a category of shapes to collect: shapes of people in paintings or sculpture, curved and rounded shapes, angular and sharp shapes, flower shapes, or another category. Take photos (where allowed) or make sketches of the different shapes you find. Talk about the different shapes and which ones are your favorites. Notice which artists seem particularly interested in shape.
- Make sculpture the focus of your museum visit. Count how many ways different artists made human body shapes in their sculptures. Make a collection of photos or sketches as you look for sculpture shapes.
- Notice shapes in abstract paintings and decorative arts. Record in sketches and photos.
- Make a collection of the different kinds of circles, squares, or triangles you see in the paintings and sculptures.
- When you find a painting or sculpture that is particularly interesting, make a list of shape words that describe it. Talk about how different shapes might communicate different emotions and feelings with visual information.

Play with Shape
- Before going to see a particular exhibit of works by an artist of note, look at pictures on the Internet or in a reference book, and talk with your child about the way the artist uses shape. What does your child notice about how the artist uses shape? Use tracing paper to trace key shapes in the pictures, or if you have a drawing program that imports photos, take a screen shot, and let your child draw over the shapes he or she notices.
- At the museum, make your body into the shapes you see, or trace the shapes in the air.

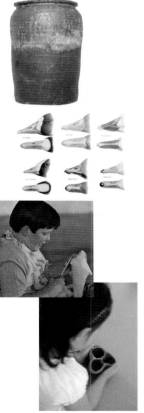

Select, Create, and Make Shape
Back at home:
- Challenge your child to sculpt shapes from playdough that communicate different moods and emotions.
- Make sculptures inspired by your art museum visit with different shape-making materials: blocks, clay, boxes and cardboard, dough, wood scraps, stuffed fabric shapes, stuffed socks with rubber bands and strings, knit fabric strips knotted and wrapped around wire, etc.
- Make a simple shape book full of photocopied duplicates of the same shape. Assemble the shape pages into a book (loose leaf or stapled), and let your child turn each page into a different drawing.
- Read some shaped poetry together. (One good book is *Come to My Party and Other Shape Poems,* by Hideko Takahashi and Heidi Roemer.) Then try to write a shaped poem of your own using the words you collected during your museum visit.

Shape

- Make a slide show or other multimedia presentation about an artist that your child likes, focusing on shape and other Sensory Alphabet information.
- Cut, paste, paint, and draw using favorite shapes from your trip to the museum. After looking at the work of a famous artist such as Calder, Arp, Miro, Picasso, or Matisse, try working in the same style. (For even young children who love shape, this can be a fun challenge.)

Special Activity: Shape at the Science Museum _____

Collect Shape

- Choose one specific exhibit, such as the shell exhibits at a science museum or the simple machine exhibits at a technology museum, and explore that exhibit for shapes. Be sure your child has a chance to find and notice shapes, using a digital camera or a sketchbook as a collection tool.
- Notice how different kinds of insects, animals, plants, shells, fossils, or other collections are distinguished by their shapes. Talk about why each animal or plant might be shaped the way it is.

Play with Shape

- Trace the shapes you see in the air with your arm or hand.
- Find shapes that are similar to one another in two or more different exhibits in the museum.

Select, Create, and Make Shape

Back at home:

- Cut or tear a collection of shapes inspired by a museum visit for children to use in collages—for example, machine parts (gears, levers, and ramps) for children to collage into their own machine inventions, or different shapes of parts of automobiles for children to reassemble into their own auto inventions.
- Make your own mini-museum at home, categorizing leaves from the backyard, rocks from a hike, shells from the beach, or other collections by shape.
- Take up ornithology, botany, or another categorical field study with your child, starting with an interest you pick up from museum visits. The library, the bookstore, and the Internet offer many resources, such as field guides targeted for beginners of any age. Any study of this kind builds shape recognition and distinction as you learn to identify species, see categories, and contrast and compare examples.

- Build a more permanent collection space in your home that honors one of your child's favorite ways to collect. Learn to press leaves, to identify shells or fossils, to capture and mount insects. Help your child make a "museum" space in his or her room.
- Make a study of origami, turning flat pieces of paper into shaped objects, animals, and more. For inspiration, here is a related video animation on the metamorphosis of a cube at http://erikdemaine.org/metamorphosis/. The documentary film *Between the Folds* is a must-see for any origami lover.

Reflect _____

- Of all the shape activities you tried, which ones were your child's favorites?
- Did any of these shape activities spark an "aha" moment?
- Do you think your child has a special affinity for shape?
- Could your child benefit from communications, routines, and daily structures that use shapes to organize or emphasize information?
- How does your sense of shape match or not match that of your child?
- Where and how and when could using clear and defined shapes, both literally and figuratively, make your everyday life more harmonious or more interesting?

Shape: Field Notes

Light

Light

Light Words

dark, bright,
sparkle,
glittery, gloom,
sunrise, sunset,
twilight, dingy,
brilliant, dim,
laser, metallic,
sizzling, contrast,
shadowy,
shimmery,
foggy, muted,
translucent,
transparent,
opaque, glint,
gleam, blinding,
incandescent,
fluorescent,
halogen,
ambient,
spotlight, stark,
floodlight,
sun, reflection,
iridescent,
flash, star,
moon, visibility,
shaded,
radiate,
pinpoint

Range

Light provides a sense of emotion, no matter where or when we are. Light is the most ephemeral of all the elements.

Description

Light, the energy element, fills our days and punctuates our nights. Perhaps the least concrete "filter" for our perceptions, light is a creative, generative tool that is wielded less often than some other tools—unless, of course, you are a photographer, theater designer, or filmmaker. However, it is always around us, affecting our mood, coloring our perception of objects and environments, or (in its absence) making nonvisual information all the more important.

Light can be direct, reflected, diffused, filtered, or blocked. Transparency, translucence, and opacity are part of the qualities of all materials, and those qualities are determined by light. Our eyes detect and reflect light. Color would not exist without it. Light can be imitated by clever painters, and captured on film and through digital media. As we spend more time in front of screens, we spend more time in media that is all about light.

Light symbolizes understanding, bright ideas, hope, happiness, what is most important . . . and "enlightenment."

Connections

- A web designer works with light-driven color and form.
- Light sets the mood for photographers and cinematographers.
- Physicists study the properties and nature of light.
- Astronomers are concerned with light as it is generated and reflected, and as it travels through space and time.
- Painters mimic the qualities of light as it creates depth, contour, and mood.
- Sculptors think about how light works with and against their sculptures.
- Inventors puzzle out new ways to create, harness, and store energy as light.
- Biologists study the effects of light on behavior, movement, cell growth, plant ecology, and countless other organic activities.
- Optometrists and ophthalmologists study light and vision, the eye, and diseases of the eye.
- Geologists focus on fluorescence, crystal reflection, and refraction.
- Botanists and gardeners know which plants need sunlight and which need shade.

The Key Question

What enlightens life for you?

Looking for Light

Materials and Objects for Exploring and Playing with Light
- windows
- cameras of all kinds
- shadow puppets
- flashlights and glow lights
- fireflies in a bottle
- campfires and firework displays
- telescope
- overhead projector or slide projector and screen for shadow and light play
- colored gels and cellophane
- plastics and films and other materials that are transparent, translucent, and reflective
- light table
- light peg board games and tools
- kaleidoscopes and taleidoscopes (kaleidoscopes without the colored pieces inside)
- sequins, glitter, glass pellets, and other materials from the crafts store
- 3-D glasses and movies
- magnifying lenses

Light

Talking about Light

She has always been there, my darling. / She is, in fact, exquisite. / Fireworks in the dull middle of February / and as real as a cast-iron pot. —Anne Sexton

All the means of action—the shapeless masses—the materials—lie everywhere about us. What we need is the celestial fire to change the flint into the transparent crystal, bright and clear. That fire is genius. —Henry Wadsworth Longfellow

Moonlight is sculpture. —Nathaniel Hawthorne

Awareness of the stars and their light pervades the Koran, which reflects the brightness of the heavenly bodies in many verses. The blossoming of mathematics and astronomy was a natural consequence of this awareness. —Fatima Mernissi

Most people would guess that the sun is fifty or a hundred times brighter than the moon, but it's a half million times brighter—evidence of the amazing capacity of our eyes to adjust to light and dark. —James Elkins

And light has no weight, / Yet one is lifted on its flood, / Swept high, / Running up white-golden light-shafts, / As if one were as weightless as light itself— / All gold and white and light. —Lawren Harris

- metallic paints and pens
- *Moongame* and other books by Frank Asch
- astronomy programs and apps such as Star Walk
- NASA's website, http://www.nasa.gov/,with photos from the Hubble and other space voyages

Light at Home and In Your Neighborhood

Collect Light

- Collect light and shadow with a digital camera. Some categories to collect include shiny things, transparent things, bright lights, dim lights, big and little shadows, shadows that make textures, shadows that make shapes, light shining through materials, light reflecting off other materials, shadows people make, shadows plants make, and light and shadow on buildings and houses.
- Which places in your home have the most interesting qualities of light? Which places in your neighborhood?
- Using paper and black markers or crayons, trace shadows that you find.
- Find the moon every night, and draw and write about what you see.
- At different times of day, trace your shadow with chalk on the driveway or sidewalk.
- Watch a TV film, movie, or stage performance, and then talk about the qualities of light and shadow. How did the director, cinematographer, and designers use light?

Play with Light

- Darken a room, and using different light-creating tools, see what you can discover. Use big and little flashlights, glow sticks, a projector, a desk lamp, and (with supervision) a candle.
- Draw and paint a picture using only black, white, and gray paints or markers.
- Play with powerful flashlights next to a body of

water—a lake, a pond, the ocean, or a swimming pool, at dusk or in full darkness. What kinds of reflections can you make?
- Investigate light with mirrors, binoculars, telescopes, and other tools.

Light

Select, Create, and Make Light

- Make a study of light sources in the sky. (Note: Parent, warn your children never to look directly at the sun!) Investigate on the web and/or read about what makes eclipses, comets, sunlight, sunspots, and other astronomical phenomena.
- Dissect a cow's eye. (For information and a video, see http://www.exploratorium. edu/learning_studio/cow_eye/) or try a virtual dissection at http://www.escho-olonline.com/company/examples/eye/eyedissect.html.
- Make a time-lapse animation of light changing in your garden or street. Set up a tripod with a still or movie camera and mark the place. Every half hour from dawn to dark, take a few frames or a few photos from the same position. Put your images together to make a slide show or movie animation. For an excellent example, see http://vimeo.com/35080048. Search the Internet for more with "time lapse photography" as a search term.
- Write a poem or song about the quality of light in your room or at the breakfast table, on a spring morning or in wintertime.

Light at the Zoo
Collect Light

- Notice what kinds of light different animals like and need. What animals are nocturnal? Which ones are light-lovers?
- Visit the zoo at night when your local zoo offers the opportunity. See how nighttime behavior and activity differs from a daytime visit.
- Can you find any fish, reptiles, or other animals whose bodies have unusual qualities of light reflection or fluorescence?
- Take photographs and make sketches of the light qualities you see at the zoo— shadows, reflections, shimmery and glittery surfaces, iridescent feathers, and shiny hooves.

Play with Light

- Observe animals through binoculars, taleidoscopes, and "lookers" made with different colored cellophane. (Note: A taleidoscope can be made from three mirrors. Put them face down, side by side, a centimeter apart, and put duct tape across all their backs. Fold them into a three-dimensional figure with the mirror faces inside. Tape the opening together. When you look through the taleidoscope, you will see a pattern of reflected images of the world around you.)
- Notice the shadows that different animal bodies make.

Select, Create, and Make Light

Back at home, use the ideas, photos, and drawings you collected at the zoo for one or more of these light projects:

- Use a shoebox to make a model diorama of an animal that likes the night and what kind of nighttime environment it lives in.
- Turn your photos of light into a slide show or animation with the theme of "light and shadow."
- Draw an animal on construction paper. Poke holes around its outline and hang in a window to see the light coming through the holes.
- Using a sheet hung in front of a doorway, with a strong light behind it, make animal shadow puppets with cardboard and sticks. Or use your own body to make animal shadow shapes, adding hats, horns, wigs, tails, and other costume pieces to change your shadow into that of an animal.

Light

Light at the Art Museum

Collect Light

- Visit the sculpture gallery or garden, and notice how light reflects, models, and makes the 3-D art more interesting. Take photos to capture the light and shadows you see.
- Look for light sculptures or other art that uses light as a material either directly or indirectly (such as stained glass, shiny glass, jewels, or glazes).
- Notice how painters from different periods in art history and different art movements capture and play with light: *chiaroscuro* (use of dark and light) in the work of painters such as Rembrandt, Caravaggio, and Vermeer; impressionism whose principal theme was light like Monet; pointillism, demonstrated in the work of Seurat; and contemporary artists interested in light, like Rothko, Turrell, and Bell.
- Visit the photography exhibits and galleries. How do different photographers use light?

Play with Light

- See how your shadow interacts with sculptures and spaces in the museum.
- Notice the lighting in the museum. Why it is placed where it is? What kind of mood do the lights create? Is some of the lighting controlled to protect old paintings or other materials?

Select, Create, and Make Light

- Back at home, make your own light paintings.
- Take photos of "light paintings" or "light graffiti" using flashlights, neon flares, or other light sources in a dark room or at night. With a long exposure with your camera, move the lights around, drawing in space.
- Build a night-light or light sculpture for your bedroom. Use colored cellophane, glass, plastic, craft materials, and glittery surfaces. Or glue fluorescent stars or paint a glow-in-the-dark scene on the wall or ceiling.
- Investigate some of the characteristics of light and color. How do light color and pigment color differ? What happens when you mix colored lights? Colored pigments?

Special Activity: Investigations with Light and Photography

Collect Light

- Document a day in your life by taking a photo every fifteen or thirty minutes. Always think about the quality and mood of the light, and make it match your mood and activity.
- Look at photographs by famous photographers: Ansel Adams, Henri Cartier-Bresson, Annie Leibovitz, Dorothea Lange, and Lennart Nilsson, for example.
- Look at photos that changed the world: http://www.worldsfamousphotos.com/ (Note: Some of these photos depict violent or disturbing images.)
- Watch an early black-and-white silent movie.

Play with Light

- Using a digital camera, photograph a still life of favorite objects under different light conditions.
- Experiment with your camera to see how much exposure it takes to make a light painting. Make light exposures of light drawings using a flashlight in a dark room, sparklers at night, or glow sticks.
- Experiment with some of the many photo-altering software filters or apps that

are available. Some apps to try: PerfectPhoto, Zapp PhotoPad for iPad, and Instagram.
- Take panoramas (long-range perspectives) and microphotos (extreme close-ups) of interesting objects, scenes, and people. One easy-to-use panorama app for iPhone is Photosynth.

Select, Create, and Make Light
- Make a pinhole camera and a simple darkroom to develop the photos taken with it. For instructions, see http://www.kodak.com/global/en/consumer/ education/lessonPlans/pinholeCamera/pinholeCanBox.shtml, http://www. diyphotography.net/23-pinhole-cameras-that-you-can-build-at-home, or other sources on the web.
- Capture a special light event on film, such as a starry night, a fireworks display, a roaring bonfire, or a candlelit dinner. How can you manipulate your camera controls to capture the light quality?
- Print and frame (or otherwise display) the most interesting photographs taken by your child. You can order prints online in numerous sizes and formats, from books to posters.
- Make your own silent movie—in black-and-white, if possible.
- Use your camera to invent or document a photo story about something or someplace you visit or imagine visiting.

Reflect

- Of all the light activities you tried, which ones were your child's favorites?
- Do you think your child has a special affinity for light, for photography, or for movie making?
- Could your child benefit from the use of light to help set a mood or to send a message?
- Is photography a tool that would help your child communicate with others when words are difficult or frustrating?
- How does your sense of light match or not match that of your child?
- Where and how and when could using light consciously make your everyday life more harmonious or more interesting?

Light: Field Notes

Write | Paste | Draw

Sound

Sound

Sound Words

ding, slurp,
frizz, fizz, zipper,
plop, ping, grrrr,
growl, sing, slap,
clap, clang,
dingle, chime,
chant, choir,
roar, tone, note,
chord, loud,
soft, vibrato,
staccato, mezzo,
soprano, alto,
bass, guitar,
viola, synthesizer,
moog,
midrange,
screech, slur,
symphonic,
whisper, shout,
speak, laugh,
cough, blip,
bling, blabber,
jabber, trill,
splat, silent, sing,
crash, clank,
gulp, click, tsk,
hmmm, um,
sigh, puff, patter,
humph, hum

Range
Sound is invisible, except in its effects, and, sometimes, at its origins. Nevertheless, sound envelops and surrounds us.

Description
Sound gives us communication, communion, and an invisible bath that cushions, directs, affects, and emanates from our emotions and actions. We make sound, we hear sound, we even feel sound. We perceive sound caused by vibrations in the air or the environment. Sometimes sound connotes meaning, as in, "I don't like the sound of that!" or "That sounds great to me." People talk, laugh, groan, yell, pop, click, clap, snap, sigh, mutter, and trill. Animals roar and low and tweet and grunt and hiss. Other sounds are by-products of activity and may soothe, irritate, or inspire. Sounds can be loud or soft, fast or slow, high or low; they can be made by plucking, rubbing, strumming, or striking. Sound stretches invisible wires between us and around us.

People stay plugged into music and conversations and news and other sounds as they go about their daily lives. They sound off about the things they care about, they speak their minds, and they even have looks that speak louder than words. Sound influences our emotions, and we respond quickly to growls, honks, or shouts—and to whispers, purrs, and chortles. And sometimes, our favorite sound is silence.

Connections
- A concert musician combines sound, performance, and mastery.
- The conductor weaves sounds together.
- A film director uses sound to carry us forward.
- Scientists study sounds in nature, machines, and humans, using sound to diagnose, treat, and repair.
- Linguists track language through sound and image.
- Psychologists hear our stories and help us to hear them, too.
- Poets find the right sounds for their words.
- Painters, novelists, and composers—all are artists who look for their own voice in their work.
- Doctors use body sounds to diagnose what's going on inside us.
- Environmentalists notice what sounds are and aren't around us.
- Machinists know the sound of a well-oiled machine.
- Sound waves tell us about tumors, earthquakes, ocean-dwellers, and structures.
- An auctioneer uses sound to build sales and to keep things moving.
- Radio announcers use their voice to paint pictures in the minds of their listeners.
- All of us use sound to communicate with others in our work and play.

The Key Question
What is your voice in your work?

Looking for Sound
Materials and Objects for Exploring and Playing with Sound
- recordings of music and natural sounds
- rattles and things to make rattles with
- books on tape
- poetry readings
- interesting sound makers from different cultures
- piano
- flute
- guitar, banjo, and/or ukulele
- clickers
- digital recorder

Sound

Talking about Sound

I will speak to you in stone-language / (Answer with a green syllable) / I will speak to you in snow-language / (Answer with a fan of bees) / I will speak to you in water-language / (Answer with a canoe of lightning), I will speak to you in blood language, (Answer with a tower of birds). —Octavio Paz

For most of us, it's revolutionary to find out that listening to or making music is not just for fun or to make you smarter, but can make you better at what you do. The systems that are enhanced by music seem to be endless. —Eric Jensen

Music is the effort we make to explain to ourselves how our brains work. We listen to Bach transfixed because this is listening to a human mind. —Lewis Thomas

My personal hobbies are reading, listening to music, and silence. —Edith Sitwell

If you develop an ear for sounds that are musical it is like developing an ego. You begin to refuse sounds that are not musical and that way cut yourself off from a good deal of experience. —John Cage

If you stand still outside you can hear it . . . winter's footsteps, the sound of falling leaves. —Takayuki Ikkaku

- digital sound toys and software apps, such as Bloom, Matrix Music Mixer (http://www.sembeo.com/media/Matrix.swf), and Raindrop Melody Maker (http://www.lullatone.com/blog/wp-content/uploads/2009/04/raindrop.swf)
- digitally simulated video—for example, this YouTube video about how a guitar might look from the inside: http://www.youtube.com/watch?v=TKF6nFzpHBU
- websites about sound, such as sound effects master Fred Newman's: http://mouthsounds.info/
- CD compilations such as *Shake It to the One That You Love the Best,* compiled by Cheryl Warren Mattox, or *De Colores and Other Latin-American Folk Song for Children,* selected by José-Luis Orozco
- books about sound, like *Read Joyful Noise, Poems for Two Voices* by Paul Fleischman, and *Desert Voices* by Byrd Baylor and Peter Parnall

Sound at Home and In Your Neighborhood

Collect Sound

- Take a "sound walk" (blindfolded with a partner to lead you) in your home and around the neighborhood. How many sounds can you hear? What do they tell you?
- Record sounds with a recorder, smartphone, or computer.
- Make a collection of CDs or a digital collection of interesting sounds and music to play in the car or when waiting in line. Use headphones with a splitter so you and your child can listen to the same recording. (Note: Use caution with sound level, especially with young ears.)

Play with Sound

- Using a small stick as a drumstick tap various objects around the table, house, or yard to see how

many sounds you can make. Try using metal, plastic, and wood sticks. Do they make different sounds?
- How many sounds can you make just with your body—mouth, hands, feet, breath? For ideas, read and listen to *Mouth Sounds* by Fred Newman, or watch his videos on YouTube.
- Tell a story just with sound.
- Listen to spoken word recordings: poetry, chants, stories. Look for books and stories that use alliteration, rhyme, or onomatopoeia, such as *The Great Kapok Tree* by Lynne Cherry or *Why Mosquitos Buzz in People's Ears* by Verna Aardema.

Sound

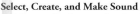

Select, Create, and Make Sound
- Make up a kitchen-pan band with your child and some friends. Play along with music, then make up your own. (Use earplugs if you must!)
- Make a sound mobile with recycled "beautiful trash." Hang it where you can hear the wind play music throughout the day.
- Make a bottle, jar, and water harmonica to play a before-dinner sonata.
- Learn how to make simple musical instruments, such as a rubber band guitar or a bamboo flute. Instructions can be found on many Internet sites, but this one links you to many others: www.rhythmweb.com/homemade/index.html
- Paint while listening to music. Change the kind of music often.

Sound at the Zoo

Collect Sound
- Use your laptop, smartphone, or a digital recorder to collect animal sounds.
- Take turns leading each other on a "sound walk," blindfolded, so that you can each concentrate on the information you discover with your ears.

Play with Sound
- Imitate the sounds you hear at the zoo, as you visit the different animals.
- Listen to what people around you have to say about the animals while they are visiting the zoo. Do you hear any similarities between people's voices and animal sounds?
- Have a conversation using the kinds of sounds you hear animals make. Pretend you are having an argument, or gossiping, or giving orders. What animal sounds best match what kind of message?

Select, Create, and Make Sound
Back at home, use the sounds you collected for these projects.
- Listen to an animal sound, and then paint a picture that expresses what the animal sounds like, as well as what it looks like. What colors, lines, and shapes do you use?
- Learn to use a sound editing program (like GarageBand, a software application that is included with Apple computers), and turn your collection into a zoo symphony. Or make a composition about something more specific, such as a song about African animals and their world of sound.

Special Activity: Sound Excursions

Embark on sound excursions, especially with children who really love sound. Here are some places to go and things to do:

- *An art museum.* Look for paintings, sculptures, and other artworks that have qualities of sound in their visual presentation. Back at home, paint while listening to different kinds of music, or make paintings of different sounds, like that of a yell, a whisper, a gentle breeze in the trees, a parade.

- *A baseball game.* Capture and collect sounds throughout the game with your recorder. At home, edit your recordings or try to reproduce the game with special effects.

- *The beach.* Listen to sounds of birds, water, waves, and wind. Build an instrument, such as a sound mobile, drum, or set of rattles from beachcombing finds —shells, driftwood, beach flotsam, and jetsam—by taking along a drill, fishing line, a couple of boards (if your beach does not provide such).

- *An orchestral performance.* Many symphonic orchestras present special concerts for families. Prepare older children for an adult performance by talking about the story of the music, the instruments, and the composer. Listen ahead of time to some short presentations. Children might enjoy drawing and writing in a sketchbook about the sounds they hear during the performance. Do the same for other kinds of musical performances. Back at home, listen to orchestral music until you can identify all the instruments.

- *The park.* Who and what are making sounds? Can you track different sounds to their sources? Be a sound detective: Find the bird, the branch, the person, the roller skates, the evidence of wind and water in the environment. Visit the park at different times of day and different times of the year. How do the sounds change? Make a calendar or chart of sounds you hear.

- *Internet/classical radio.* Listen to radio shows from the 1920s to 1950s, such as *Abbott and Costello, The Shadow, Gunsmoke,* and *Orson Welles's Mercury Theatre.* Try haunted house sounds (http://www.youtube.com/watch?v=wAMTi4e3cr4). Also, listen to funny music and sounds like those of Spike Jones or Victor Borge. Investigate different singers singing difficult pieces, such as Mozart's "Queen of the Night" (http://www.youtube.com/watch?v=aLwKnFBnATo&feature=related) or Roy Rogers yodeling (http://www.youtube.com/watch?v=u00Y11x16V0&feature=fvst). Create your own shows with funny or unusual or scary sounds.

Reflect

- Of all the sound activities you tried, which ones were your child's favorites?
- Do you think your child has a special affinity for sound, music, or a particular instrument?
- Could your child benefit from the use of sound to help set a mood, to signal a change of activity, or to make a task go more easily and quickly?
- Would your child benefit from music lessons because of his or her affinity for sound and music making?
- How does your sense of sound match or not match that of your child?
- Do you often play music at home or in the car? Could you make more varied and conscious choices in the music environment at home?

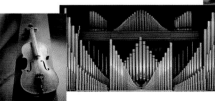

Sound: Field Notes

Write | Paste | Draw

Exploring Your Child's Creative Strengths

*"The Intuitive Mind is a sacred gift
and the Rational Mind is a faithful servant.
We have created a society that honors
the servant and has forgotten the gift."*
—*Albert Einstein*

Each child is absolutely unique. If you spend fifteen minutes watching at the playground, you'll know it. If you look at a stack of drawings by a group of six-year-olds, you'll see the differences.

It is vital for parents to notice their child's creative strengths early. Knowing and supporting a child's particular and unique strengths is a very special ingredient that parents can add to their child's development. A child's creativity will be amplified with thoughtfully selected materials, custom-designed activities, and like-minded resources. In this section, we'll give you tools for observing your child's strong suits, and ideas for resources to nurture and cultivate them.

But first, we want to give you some evidence—photographs of real kids—that show how individual differences look and how patterns of strengths show themselves in a child's creative work. Insight often comes from the contrasts you notice when comparing several children at the same time; then the differences jump to the forefront and grab your attention. The following photos and observations were made during a summer workshop course for five-year-olds, called New World Kids, at the Aldrich Contemporary Museum in Ridgefield, Connecticut, in the summer of 2007.

Seeing Imaginations at Work

There were a dozen "new world kids" participating, so, of course, there are a dozen unique stories and profiles. During the two-week course, children had the opportunity to:

- learn the Sensory Alphabet
- build observation skills
- practice the creative process
- experience a variety of media
- hear from adults about their own thinking and working processes

Along the way, we observed and noticed the children's individual differences and documented their work.

After a few days, patterns began to emerge. The Sensory Alphabet is used here as a lens to demonstrate those patterns. We've selected three children whose imaginations can be readily contrasted in print as examples for seeing differences and strengths when you look at your own child's artwork, activities, and actions. Meet these three children:

Henry is very spatially oriented, particularly in a 3-D sense. His work demonstrates this understanding: he sees and makes strong shapes. Henry is interested in balance and symmetry and repeatedly chooses to work with few shapes and colors.

Grace loves texture. Her favorite ways of working include layers and multiple media whenever possible. The tactile qualities of the materials are important, and for Gracie, more is always better.

Pedro is very visual, and his work is very linear. He loves filling 2-D graphic space with line drawings of the movies that are playing in his mind. He is also a natural storyteller—another linear format. (As a young five-year-old, he needed a secretary to record the stories that complete his work.)

The photographs on the following pages show examples of how each child approached a particular activity and what he or she "produced." These tangible objects are clues to each child's individual strengths and unique creative process. We've noted a bit about that process of work or approach that each child took, since those clues are just as important (or maybe more so) than the final product. These activities are all *open-ended*—ones that call forth personal and creative responses from the child. There are no right answers, no copying. (Open-ended activities are essential for providing these kinds of clues, because other kinds of lessons too often have an implicit right or wrong answer. You don't get the child's answer, you get the learned response.)

The First Clue

On *Space* day, the children chose small cardboard figures to represent themselves, and each created a model space for that figure, one that felt comfortable in size and shape. The media were clay and straws.

Henry

Henry quickly and intuitively created a space made with triangles. It was simple and stable and showcased his natural understanding of working with 3-D elements.

Grace

Grace created a cube, a shape that probably came more from an idea of a space— like a toy house. It was a physical representation that started with a mental con-

struct, unlike Henry's space, one constructed directly from manipulation of the materials. Grace's space was then translated (with a bit of help from an adult) into a space for her tiny pretend "self."

Pedro

Pedro "did not compute." His strong 2-D orientation made it difficult for him to even imagine a 3-D space, much less construct one. And he was not being silly or acting up. This is a vital clue to the shape of Pedro's imagination.

The Second Clue

On *Color* day, a designer visited the class; he brought colored yarns and talked about how he used color in designing clothes. He also brought an activity: designing a shirt. The children worked on a template with markers. Here are their designs and some notes about what became apparent about their individual styles:

Henry

Henry used the linear media (markers) to create shapes. He used only two colors—on purpose.

Grace

Grace created a texture design. Clearly, she could stay inside the lines if she chose (check out the pink collar), but she expressed tactile information with her wild and woolly lines.

Pedro

Pedro chose lines, his favorite element, and carefully filled the space, with no overlapping. He also included many colors.

The Third Clue

On *Texture* day, one of the activities was making collages; many materials were available to use. These three children had strikingly different responses:

Henry

Henry responded with a few hard-edged shapes. The balanced and symmetrical placement was important, and his choice of materials seemed more related to the shape of the objects than their tactile qualities.

Grace

Grace really enjoyed making a collage. She chose elements that had a strong tactile quality and then layered them. Her work was full of texture.

Pedro

Pedro's idea of a collage was more like a classification system. He placed his chosen elements in rows (lines), and nothing overlapped.

The Fourth Clue

Throughout the course, the "new world kids" worked on "me papers"—life-sized tracings of each kid that they filled in with all kinds of personal favorites, using writing or drawing. On the last day, we finished these and added paint to the available media choices. This is how they turned out:

Henry

Henry colored in his clothes as big shapes (not easy when you're working with markers) and stayed carefully inside the lines for definition. You can see from the little red shapes on his shirt that he is a Red Sox fan.

Grace

Gracie worked all over the paper and was delighted to figure out that she could slide things under the paper, making rubbings to create a textural effect. She cut out colored shapes and pasted them on, too.

Pedro

Pedro chose one area of the figure to fill with a drawing that made a story. He was happy to use markers only and liked the bright, graphic colors. (The drawing in the upper left corner shows his drafting skill.)

The Fifth Clue

On the last day, the children were allowed to select their favorite media and create whatever they wished with the supplies and tools available. The results added to the individual profiles of their unique styles of thinking and working. Their differences continued to show:

Henry

Henry created a 3-D sculpture, a strong and simple shape using three colors.

Grace

Grace's final project was a collage with many materials and layers. Here she is, at work on it with her tape in hand.

Pedro

Since Pedro was barely five and couldn't write yet, but because of his desire to tell an elaborate story, he needed an assistant for his final project. His assistant took dictation as Pedro illustrated the story with line drawings.

What the Clues Tell Us

Henry

Henry's 3-D skills and interest in balance might foreshadow an interest in architecture, engineering, or construction. To encourage his strengths to develop, a project to design and build a doghouse or a tree-house with the help of an architectural student or builder would certainly feed his mind.

Grace

Grace's love of texture needs hands-on media. Many fields accent the tactile sensibility that Gracie has in abundance—cooking, weaving, surgery, or maybe clothing design. Planning and then planting a garden with a grandparent, then cooking with the results, would be an absorbing project for Gracie.

Pedro

Pedro's very strong visual and linear imagination, paired with his drawing skill, could lead him to explore animation or possibly video game design. That same linear quality, along with his love of storytelling, might transfer to an interest in words when he goes to school; perhaps he will study writing or journalism. Learning how to storyboard with a moviemaker would feed Pedro's imagination.

Adding It All Up

The individual style of each child's pattern of thinking and creating is consistent and distinct, and it is something that will continue throughout their lifetimes. These patterns show us where their natural imaginations are most fluent and most satisfying. They also give beginning indications of what media, fields of study, and even careers the children might enjoy.

But notably, the institution of education today would most likely reward only Pedro's linear sensibility. Henry's skill with shape and space, Grace's strong textural sense—these strengths are not on the radar screen of what is important at school. There is a very real danger of these championship children being defined by an education system that recognizes only a limited set of skills and grades them according to a narrow set of strengths. For young children, identities can be at stake.

For now, this means supporting your child's individual strengths and problem-solving skills with materials and experiences that they are unlikely to find in school. As your child gets a bit older and becomes aware of and centered in her strengths, she can take more responsibility for her own learning—knowing which subjects may be more difficult and which will be a breeze. For example, a linear, 2-D kid may do well with the linear qualities of algebra but find visualizing the 3-D shapes of solid geometry more difficult. The Sensory Alphabet is a formidable tool for analyzing the qualities of fields of study and matching them with children's strengths. And also, it's a tool to bridge the gaps. For example, a child with a strong sense of movement may need to learn ways to translate math memorization tasks into movement games in order to achieve mastery.

Assessing Your Child's Strengths

This is where parents come in. You can locate your children's natural strengths, mirror them back to them, and show your child that you value these strengths—and the child himself or herself. Parents who teach creative thinking make home a place where each individual's creativity is practiced, valued, and supported.

So, how do you look at your child with new eyes, outside of the daily *get-dones* and *to-dos*? It helps to have a certain distance, an anthropologist's viewpoint, even as you make your way through a busy day. How do you step beyond easy judgments—*this is good; this is bad*—and into a position of value-free observation? How do you see what's really there?

The following pages provide a palette of questions, grouped in different categories, for parents to ask themselves about their child—ways of contrasting and comparing qualities to bring them into a higher focus—a checklist to help you observe and collect what you notice. You might want to set up a file folder, or make nightly notes on a calendar about what you observe. Start a "Me Book" with your child, where both of you record what you learn.

First, Ask Your Child

Metacognition, thinking about one's own thinking, can begin early. Even little children can tell you what they like and do not like to do. They can also describe what they see, hear, touch, and otherwise take in through their senses. So ask your child. You may be surprised at the answers. Here are some questions to start with:

- What are your favorite ways to play?
- How do you feel about reading?
- About writing? Is it easy or hard?
- What kind of puzzles do you like to solve?
- What do you like to draw? Or is drawing too hard?
- What do you daydream about?
- What would you like to act out?
- What are your favorite games?
- Sports?
- Songs?
- Do you like to dance? When, where, and how?
- What do you like to build and what would be fun to build with?
- What things are best to do with friends?
- Have you ever thought about growing plants?
- Or taking care of animals?

Older children can easily respond to inventories by listing their favorites and out-of-school activities. Ask your children about recent vacations or travel, or excursions and parties. What have been the favorites, what not-so-much? In talking to children about their likes and dislikes, make the conversation as value-free as possible. You want to hear what your kids like, not what they think you want them to like.

Observe Your Child

Start with observation. Keep your eyes open and make an effort to look with your "anthropologist's eyes." Use a camera to catch typical actions and behaviors, or just reflect and write. Use this checklist to help you develop a sense of your child's strengths, and what inspires curiosity and confidence.

- How does my child sound? What's his voice like? Do you hear the clumping or tiptoeing or trotting of her feet through space? Is this a child with soft or strong sound qualities? Is he talking fast or mulling things over before he speaks? Is she a story always in the telling, or a dramatic announcer of all things important?
- How does my child move? Is she a whirlwind at the center of any activity or a slow observer who has to watch before jumping in? Does he have wings on his feet and a kinesthetic grasp of each and every movement through space? Or is every physical activity a tug-of-war? Do you note a facility with hand-eye coordination, or do you have a kid whose favorite exercise is mental gymnastics? Does she fidget and wiggle her way through the day, daintily twirl at every opportunity, or cut through space with conviction, ignoring obstacles and rules at every turn?
- What is the rhythm of my child? If he clapped a rhythmic score, would it be regular and evenly paced? Or erratic and unpredictable? Would she be a march or a tango? A jive or a three-ring circus? Is he fast, slow, or somewhere in between? Full of surprises or forthright?
- How does my child use his or her face and eyes? Is this one an open book or a mysterious stranger who seldom lets his emotions show? Is drama the operative word or is methodical her method? What happens when your child meets a stranger? Is he out in the game or on the sideline keeping score?
- How does my child present a public face? Is it different from the private life you see as a parent? How do others respond to your child?
- What kind of roles and functions does my child take on? Alpha dog? Follower? Listener? Starring role? Backstage director? Conformist? Devil's advocate?
- What makes my child laugh? What makes her funny? Where's his funny bone? What brings her joy? What is sure to bring a smile to his face?
- What questions does my child ask over and over and over again? Is she a "What?" or a "Why?" A "How do I?" or a "What if I?" What makes his viewpoint different from anyone else's—one-of-a-kind?

Note Your Child's Preferences

Another way to collect information about your child and her strengths is to note preferences—the things she collects, chooses, concentrates her efforts on. Here's a second checklist of observations and inventories:

- What catches my child's eye? Movement? Color? Light and shadow? Strong patterns? Interesting shapes? Or is it all about touch? Or movement? Or telling the story of what's going on?
- What holds my child's attention? What things does he or she do for longer than other children? Playing or listening to music? Building and construction toys? Puzzles or books? Art making or role-playing?
- What does my child surround her- or himself with? What are his choices for toys, for his room, for activities? Does she like being around other people? Animals? Things to build with? Stuff that moves?
- What qualities do my child's favorite games and toys have? Do they take big or small movements? Do they have procedures or linear rules? Do they have strong sensuous qualities, tactile elements, or lots of sound and motion? How about emotional or analytic components?
- What does my child collect? What gets picked up on the street or on the playground? Rocks and shells? Magazines? Bugs? Little glittery bits of foil and glass? If she could make a collection of anything, would it be hats or robots, ribbons, or sports equipment? Does he find and save photos, maps, or cartoons? Character dolls or jokes?
- What kinds of things—especially in a new place or space—is my child most likely to comment about? Does he point out the people or the colors? The sound or the story? The size or the materials? The construction and engineering or the aesthetics and theatrical sense? What does she pick up? Save? Store? Ask about or comment on?

Consider Materials

What are the qualities of the materials that your child likes best? Track these favorites through the Sensory Alphabet.

Line

Do these favorite materials have a linear quality? Are they curved or angular? Strongly directional, repetitive, or meandering? Is there always a story line going on, a movie in the mind?

Rhythm

Are the materials your child chooses stacked or patterned? Put in order or grouped? Repeated or reorganized over and over? Put away in categories or lumped together any old way? Is there a rhythm to her play—a beginning, middle, and end? Do wordplay or rhymes have a particular charm?

Space

What spatial qualities do the materials have? Are these favorite materials two-dimensional or three-dimensional? Given a choice, does your child choose clay or paper and pen? What's the scale he or she likes to work with—a desktop or a playing field? Tiny miniatures or large brushes and a six-foot-tall roll of paper?

Movement

Do your child's favorite materials move or have movement implicit in them? Is there a rhythm to them or to their use? Is the movement smooth, fast, or floating? Humorous, serious, or unstable? Does your child simply have to move no matter what or where?

Texture

How do the materials your child likes feel to the touch? Are they smooth or nubby, plastic or hard, malleable or rigid, natural or man-made? Is that collection of stuffed animals a textural necessity or a cast of characters for bed-top drama?

Color

What are the color qualities of the materials that your child likes best? Are these materials colorful or monochromatic? What kinds of colors—bright or subtle? Dark or light? Contrasting or soothing? One child may have to have that new box of crayons, while another just needs a big black permanent marker.

Shape

Do these materials—toys, games, art media, favorite objects—have definite shapes? Or are they ambiguous or amorphous? Are they simple in contour or intricate? Do they have structural parts or components? Which is the ultimate entertainment: a morning in a sandbox or a day in the sand at the beach?

Light

Are these materials with special qualities of light, dark, opacity, or transparency? Does your child play with light and shadow? Does he or she like to create an environmental mood?

Sound

Do your child's favorite materials make sounds, either by design or by the way your child uses them? What kind of sound quality do they have—musical or percussive, wind or string, whistling or thudding? Is there a definite rhythm to the sound produced? Does your child make sounds with things that no one else would ever think to turn into an instrument?

Other Things to Consider

Here is a final checklist to consult as you observe, question, and take an inventory of your child's choices, actions, and preferences:

- What spaces and places does your child prefer for free play? Is she always on the porch or in her bedroom? Alone in the backyard or in the kitchen with everyone else? Does he need a run in the park now and again to stay healthy and sane? Is time alone essential? Or is time spent with a group mandatory and energizing?
- When we interact, is it playful or serious? Directive? Organized? Improvisational?
- When my child and I work together on a task, does she stay on track or need to come and go? Does he need a process or a product? Does she have to know why or why not? Does he want to know what the payoff is?
- When we play, does she want to be the boss of me? Or does she prefer to watch and follow? Is he open to coaching or resistant to change? Does she worry about getting it "right"? Is he making up new rules as you go along or sticking to a strategy?

What Next?

Take some time to "add up" the qualities you see, as we did earlier in considering the strengths of Henry, Grace, and Pedro. Begin to see your child as a mind at work. What kinds of materials would really feed this mind? What people do you know who might make wonderful mentors? What projects could really expand this child's special brand of creativity?

The next big step is to help your child grow his or her strengths. Learning to emphasize individual strengths and patterns of creative potential takes on added urgency when we consider the context in which the children of today are developing. With all we've discussed about the focus of the educational system in America today, it's plain to see that it's up to you, the parent, to foster your child's individual creativity. Mobilize materials, tools, technology, and other resources that facilitate your child's best way to play and create—in his or her own particular and original way. Here are some specific ways you can open the doors to your child's creative thinking.

1. Provide Fitting Materials

Work/play with materials can be especially important for growing young minds. If you think back to the materials you observed your child being most attracted to, then you will know which materials to provide. These materials can be recycled items, still-useful throwaways, scrounged materials, or bought supplies, as long as they suit his or her special way of thinking and working. The important thing is to match the materials to the qualities the child loves best—the kinds of *lines, rhythms, spaces, movements, textures, colors, shapes, lights,* and *sounds* that are the most satisfying.

If a child likes ...	Try giving him or her ...
LINE	Japanese brush and ink, wire scraps, yarn, string, thread, pencil, and ruler
RHYTHM	patterns and designs of all kinds, costumes and props to make up plays, a large amount of similar small objects
SPACE	boxes of all sizes, paper and tape, magazine cutouts (pages are also spaces)
MOVEMENT	space to move in, big things to whirl and twirl and flip, balls, cylinders of all sizes, rope and things for swings
TEXTURE	rusty metal, chalk, fabric scraps, cotton, straw packaging, polyfill stuffing
COLOR	paint, markers, food coloring, colored cellophane, colored paper scraps, bright felt
SHAPE	mud, clay, dough, scissors, and paper materials for stuffed animals
LIGHT	mirrors, tinfoil, glitter, sequins, sparkles
SOUND	musical instruments, recording device, CDs, digital sound software, tubes, and rattles

2. Provide Open-Ended Activities

Parents can provide custom-designed experiences that will inspire each unique imagination. Each activity should give some structure and direction, but each child must be able to make unique responses. Provide options. Open-ended activities can be as simple as making a special bookmark for Grandma, or as complicated as designing a whole birthday party. The trick is to provide activities that have a structure appropriate to your child's imagination and skills, and yet also allow for unique and special outcomes.

Use the creative process in big and little ways. Make *collecting, playing,* and *inventing* part of the activity. Then include *sharing* and *reflection.* When the activity is finished, talk over the results with your child. This is how to build metacognitive skills—teaching your child to think about how he or she thinks and learns—and the goal is to help children eventually take charge of their own learning and development. Some ideas for open-ended activities include the following:

- An open-ended reading experience. Write, draw, or act out your favorite part of the book you just read.
- An open-ended evening experience. Watch the moon each night for a week. Write or draw your observations.
- An open-ended neighborhood experience. Interview a family member and/or neighbors to find out why and how their family settled in the neighborhood. Make a book with the findings.

3. Provide Creative Guidance

Take the time to guide your child through the process of creating from an idea that is all his or her own. There might be a need your child notices or a "crazy notion" that seems too big or too daunting to imagine working on. Take the lead and assist your child's thinking—go step by step through the creative process and into an original solution. Maybe next time your child will be ready do it all on his or her own!

As a child grows older and develops an increased capacity for reflection, the subject of individual strengths can be a shared and ongoing investigation between you. It can even be a source of inspiration—for example, on a family vacation, each family member can step up when it's his or her time to shine: *Who enjoys research? Who's best at logistics? Who likes navigating? Who would do the best job at assembling the picnic basket?*

Parents can also find like-minded mentors for their children, people who can inspire them with new experiences, people with expertise in fields of study that parents know little about, particularly when your own native style doesn't match your child's. Conversely, when a child is confident and centered in his or her strengths, it can be a valuable experience to "crew" for an expert in a field that really doesn't match—to observe, try on, and try out a totally different kind of mind-set. This is a way for your child to stretch his or her mind and imagination.

Keep an eye out for opportunities with groups, teams, and clubs. Big projects, like creating an exhibition or putting on a play, present the need to call on more than one viewpoint. These are great opportunities for building skills in collaboration. Kids get to analyze how best to use one another's strengths: *Who can be the lighting director? Who does the business and takes the tickets? Who designs the costumes? Who writes the story? Who does the advertising?*

If all this sounds like a lot to think about, plan, and implement . . . it is. But as a parent, you are no stranger to finding time and resources where there seem to be none. The next section of this book will afford you some thinking tools for designing time and space to support the unfolding of each and every child's individual creative potential within the context of the everyday.

Managing for Creativity in the Context of the Everyday

"As our case is new, we must think and act anew."
—*Abraham Lincoln*

You have taken the first steps on a journey into the often confusing territory called *creativity*. It might be called Creativity 101, assuming that it is a subject that can be approached, explored, and learned. You've studied the Sensory Alphabet, another fundamental symbol system children should know as they learn to create any form and in any field. You've learned about and explored the creative process—how it functions as both a method of thinking and a way of working. You've looked into the importance of playing, and in playing with many media—a practice fundamental to educating all the senses, all the ways of knowing. You've confronted the huge subject of individuality and its bearing on personal creativity, and understand how to explore that personally, with your own child. Taken all together, this portfolio of "knowings" will become a core reference point for creating, for inventing—and importantly, for communicating with digital media. These skills and "knowings" are the beginnings of a literacy of creativity. You are building a strong mental base camp for the forays ahead.

Now it's time to take the next step, to put what you've learned into action. You've built up an understanding of the creative process and how it can benefit your child. How can you make creativity happen on an ongoing, real-world, day-by-day basis? How can parents ensure that creativity becomes a useful, even vital part of the educational legacy we want to pass on to our children?

From our base camp of creative literacy, we can launch our "everydays" into the imagination! Often our everydays just "happen." We inhabit the same twenty-four hours each day; whatever happens, happens within that frame. Time is the space we fill with *to-dos* and *tah-dahs*, tasks and tidbits, routines and rituals. Ideally, these get us through each day with grace. We accomplish what has to be done—clothes, meals, cleaning, comfort, homework, carpools, calendars, the daily juggle of work, play, and rest—and we also try to take time to nurture that unrepeatable individuality that inhabits our child. Don't let nurturing your child's creativity become just another guilt-ridden task to fit into an already squeezed-to-the-limits schedule. Design time for invention into the everyday. Taking time as a parent to actually think about and structure routines and environmental cues that support creative thinking can go a long way toward this goal.

Time spent with our children—day-to-day actions, some in-place reactions, and the occasional special celebration—is truly unrepeatable. Mindfulness and intent, as well as improvisation, carry a lot of weight for parents. Each day we face a little someone who is a little bit older, a little bit wiser, a little bit further along his or her path to independence. Along the way, we must find ways to support what is unique and special about our child's mind and creative process.

In the next pages, you'll find some formulas for shaping the everyday by exercising your own parental creativity along the way. This is by no means an all-encompassing compendium of to-dos—just a few starters to get the gears going.

Modeling Creative Thinking

Our children believe in what they see every day. What we actually do every day tells them what we parents think is important. Whatever we wish for our children will be transmitted through the medium of daily existence. Every day, for better or worse, is all we have to give our children.

If we consistently rethink and invent meaningful everydays for our children, they will learn to rethink and invent as well. If we wish our children to be creative, we ourselves must be creative. The product of our creation must be an everyday context that allows our children to exercise their creativity, an everyday whose pattern expresses a creative process.

Nurturing creative thought is an overlay, an attitude, and a willingness to seize opportunities on the fly. It is also the everyday act of making careful, conscious choices about how we spend our time as a family. If every night is spent in front of one screen or another, if the default during "downtime" is to turn on the cell and check for messages, if shopping is our only recreation, we are sending messages about the place and value of creative thought and action—namely, that there is no place for it or value in it. These messages will far outweigh the expensive after-school lessons or summer camps that many parents hope will encourage creativity in their children.

If your first reaction to this suggestion is, "But I'm not creative," reflect back to your own childhood. Is there some activity, skill, or interest you recall that you can add back into your life, sharing it with your child? Even if it's not something you can do together, creative activity that you honor for yourself sends a powerful message about its value. If you like to write, write. If you sew, set up a sewing studio. The Internet is filled with DIY and make-it instructions for a world of activities, from simple to sophisticated. Get out there and try something new; if it's age appropriate, enlist your child's help with something that is engaging for both of your minds and hands.

Think about the creative aspects of your vocation, whether you spend your time in paid or unpaid work, and share that with your child, too. Use the Sensory Alphabet as a vocabulary to talk about what you do. For example, if you cook creatively, involve your child with simple tasks, and talk about your creative decision making with color, texture, and flavor. Take your child to work if you can. Children are hungry for reality, and not just the version on TV. Think back to your own childhood; remember how much you wanted to grow up so you could do "real" stuff.

If you have a very different set of strengths from your child's (and that happens more often than not), consider who in your family or circle of friends may share a creative streak with your child. Imagine you are booking an interview guest for your child's talk show: *Who would you want her to meet? What kind of professions or careers would be good for him to know more about? Who in your circle of friends and colleagues would be open to sharing creative thinking in his or her field with your child?*

Building Routines from Individual Strengths

Not every routine works for every child. Understanding your child's individuality—his or her strengths, cycles, and concerns—can help shape routines and rituals that keep the wheels turning more easily. Using what you have discovered about your child's individuality can help you match form (of thought patterns and perceptions) to function (getting the job done).

Consider these questions and opportunities in order to build routines that work for you and your child:

- Are transitions always an issue? What could be designed as "warning bells" or "countdowns" if your child has problems making shifts from one activity to another? Does taking a break from a task to run, skip, or jump help? Or does your child need a chance to stop, look, and listen?

- Kids love secret signals and signs. What kind of signal can be designed ahead of time—a gesture, a word, a phrase—to stand in for one of those parental warnings? Make this secret language an invention project among the family. Use a signal that your child will notice based on his or her communication strengths.
- How could you honor your child's strong suits in daily tasks such as cleaning up toys, making the bed, taking part in meal preparations, getting homework done? A child with a strong sense of rhythm might enjoy timed tasks or racing the clock; a child who responds to space probably needs well-defined places to put things and a special area for homework tasks. A child who loves color and shape could take on the dinner table as an art project (just make sure the cleanup is part of the deal). A child with a strong sense of line might enjoy coming up with a procedure to follow and a checklist with stickers for marking off tasks.
- What kinds of chores really make sense for your child's mind? Don't let what you think is age- or gender-appropriate overshadow a child's real abilities and interests. If your child loves small-motor work and is competent with tools, add more sophisticated cooking tasks. If he loves big movement, turn him loose on raking the yard or cleaning windows with a long-handled squeegee. If she's detail oriented, make her the official keeper-of-the-calendar. Find real work, not make-work, for children to do.
- What kinds of bedtime rituals fit your life and your child? How could this be a special time for communication in a way that honors individuality? Bedtime could mean storytelling together, poems read, music for the mood, slow stretches—depending on a child's strong suits.

Tackle other day-to-day tasks by inventorying the materials at hand, your family goals, and whether the task needs to go on autopilot or offers room inside of it for your child to exercise his or her creative imagination. Take time to shape the day-to-day routines that make up your everyday. Your everyday is the material you have to work with; learning to create your best ones can be a skill your child takes with him or her throughout a lifetime.

Here are two fresh approaches for establishing routines and daily rituals that honor your child's sense of innovation:

1. By-Laws for Everyday Living

Imagine working out the details of everyday maintenance completely before-hand—and submitting it to group approval and input. To be included in these "by-laws," something must be absolutely essential to everyday upkeep—necessary to do again and again repeatedly to keep the family running smoothly. The laws should allow functions to change, however, and should not specify who does what, but rather should cover the *quality* of everyday maintenance and its *execution*. In this way, you draft a document designed to meet your family's needs, express your values, and realize some of your hopes simultaneously.

What if:
- We equate cleaning with care or exquisite craftsmanship?
- Cooking becomes a creative everyday activity?
- Preparations of all kinds become moments to reflect, not rush?
- Family members make a point to notice and honor each other's homecomings?
- We pause five seconds before answering one another, to consider a new and refreshing response?
- We don't expect any one person to be "in charge" of the house?

By-laws for everyday living can be a stabilizing element in the everyday, bridging the gap between what we want the everyday to be and what it must contain.

2. On-the-Go Policies

This time, assume that your family will is not always able to work out all the details of an everyday design all at once. Most of your time will be spent in getting through the day rather than planning how to make the most of it all. Or, perhaps your family finds it hard to change everything at once and needs to concentrate on changing one thing at a time. Whatever the reasons, sometimes it is best to devise on-the-go policies for everyday living. This means your family will generally be responding spontaneously to what occurs every day, but you will be fortified by some prior decisions about what tack to take when certain situations arise. For example, what kinds of things can you imagine doing to handle bad feelings, boredom, emergency, physical problems, unmet expectations, and interruptions of plans?

What if:
- We decide beforehand how to respond to arguments within the family?
- We make a suggestion box of things to do when we feel bad or see someone else feeling bad?

- We make a to-do list of things to do when boredom sets in?
- We organize the information we might need for various kinds of emergencies and put them where we can get to them quickly?
- We make a policy to always listen and ask questions before we decide?
- We let other people solve their own arguments and refuse to get involved?

On-the-go policies force us to declare boundaries beforehand so that we know when to say yes, when to say no, and when to change to another direction.

Home: A Place for Ideas

Often, it seems, we buy into a prepackaged idea about what a home is and what it should look like, an idea sold to us through glossy magazines and TV shows, reinforced by culture and class, limited or expanded by budget, and sometimes, greatly frustrating for everyday life with kids. Our ideas of home are often designed for appearance rather than creative thought and activity.

Here are some tips that give you permission to make your home work for you—to make it work for creativity.

Make Space for Collections

As you've seen, collecting is an essential component of the creative process. Collections can take all manner of shape and form, but for most, some kind of physical (or at least digital) space is essential in order for the collection to nudge our brains into connections and creativity. Consider the following ways to rethink spaces in your home that are more conducive to collecting:

- Where can your child save, share, and catalog his or her Sensory Alphabet collections? Try little pinboards, wall-sized bulletin boards, collection cubbies, shelves, a pedestal or shadowbox for changing displays, and other special areas. Clear, plastic shoeboxes are good for small items and categorizing.
- Honor each person's collections in revolving "exhibits" throughout your home.
- Think digitally. Schedule a photo-sharing night for digital collection reviews, or buy an inexpensive digital photo frame to share a child's collection of lines, shapes, or colors. Set up an area on the family computer for each person's photo collection. Take time to make periodic photo books either with your own printouts or using an online photo book program like Shutterfly or Blurb.

Make Space for Media and Play

As you design your home, choose furnishing for children's rooms, and organize spaces for your child's play in the home, pay more attention to what's really going on—or to what needs to go on—rather than to what a decorator might suggest.

- Themed bedrooms and playrooms may be popular, but make sure the theme has something to do with your child's imagination. Most kids need a space for messy play, whether outdoors or in. Many children need ways to move differently within their living spaces. Some kids need specialized spaces for collections, for tools, for building toys or costumes.
- Make it easy for you (and your child) to clean up, to keep tools organized, to allow some controlled clutter or materials and media. Can you dedicate a closet to arts and crafts materials? Build an outside cabinet for balls, sports equipment, and outdoor tools? Provide aprons or designate work clothes that your child knows are good for messy work? If space permits, have an outdoor cleanup space for making those messy transitions back into the house—a mud room, a covered porch with storage, even an outdoor shower.
- If some home areas need to serve multiple functions (for example, the dining table for study and creative crafts, as well as eating) invent storage, conversion, disposal, and protection systems that make transitions easy. For example, a heavy-duty plastic tablecloth over a felt protector can keep a table surface safe. Consider laying out roll-up canvas drop cloths from the home remodeling store to keep floors clean. Large plastic bins with lids and wheels can make cleanup easier. It really is easier to initiate work/play and then return to square one if everything has a place. Discard, recycle, or pass along toys, tools, materials, and other stuff that your family no longer uses; this will make space for the things you do use.
- The digital nation needs some specialized boundaries, too. Many families choose to have a family computer in a space that is easy to monitor for appropriate use. Consider monitoring software or selective blocking depending on your child's age. Also, take time to discuss and explore the Internet and various websites with your child, developing media literacy skills as you go. On the hard drive, create an organizational system that works for everyone in the family, and be sure that kids know what software, folders, and documents are appropriate for their use. As to the physical aspects of digital tools, make a space for storing cords, discs, and external drives—and designate best practices for use with your child.

Make Space for Minds at Work

Design your child's room as space for a mind at work. Plan and build it together, keeping these tips in mind:

- Does your child need room to move and levels to move through? Does he need lots of table space and a wall-mounted roll of three-foot-wide paper for drawing? Does she need a hard surface for building toys and construction sets? Does he need lots of pegs and hangers for a collection of hats and costumes for dramatic play? Should there be a stage? What kind of books and media need to be at hand? What kind of raw materials and tools?
- Look through school furnishing and school supply catalogs for ideas and resources beyond the department store children's furnishings. Often, these are less expensive and more durable. Inexpensive possibilities can be found at thrift stores and reclaimed building material outlets. If you're handy, DIY with wooden crates, boards and bricks, recycled barrels, or sturdy cardboard cartons from the grocery warehouse.
- Investigate outdoor options. Whether you have a large yard, a pocket-sized garden space, or just a balcony, investigate the options to fit your child's imagination and opportunity for invention. What if you invented wind chimes, suncatchers, a treehouse, or a sandbox or sandtable? An obstacle course or game field? A secret hiding spot, an outdoor stage, a camping tent, and a fire pit?

Make Space for Sharing Creative Work

Where do you put all the products of a creative mind (or two)? What does your child make and invent? Let's face it, the refrigerator door-and-magnet-system, while easy to maintain, has a certain limited prestige. Think about what your child makes and invents and the final forms that result. What is the best and most convenient way to showcase his or her work? Here are some suggestions for honoring creative work, without having to rent a storage unit to save it all:

- Three words: digital, digital, digital. Take photos, videos, and audio records of work your child does at home, at school, and in other programs and classes. Set a weekly documentation time for taking shots and discarding (most of) the original work. Let your child pick and choose what gets saved into an annual (physical) portfolio—or transformed into the next level of creative form. As your child gets older and more skilled with digital media, he or she can select, edit, and make digital records to share.
- Have a commercial poster print made of a collection of your child's art—one

poster can reproduce a grid of smaller images of art (scanned or photographed from the original construction paper) or even thumbnail images of a slew of art and inventions. This could be a monthly or a seasonal project. Or for a do-it-yourself version, take and print snapshots of artwork, crop into squares, and tape or glue to a piece of posterboard or foamcore board.

- Specify a hallway or alcove as the family gallery space. Buy easy-to-use frames and/or shadowboxes in one or several sizes. Change out the art, photos, and artifacts that are displayed monthly or seasonally.
- Consider using the dinner table as a changing collection exhibition space, with different family members as curators for a night, a week, or once a week for a month.
- Establish a "museum shelf" in a corner of the house to display the entire family's best accomplishments for the week.

Going Pro

When time and resources permit, consider taking your child's inventions and creative work to the next stage of professional production. These works of art and imagination can become part of a child's room, the family room décor, or an outdoor installation in the garden. Try these ideas to take it to the next level:

- Use a child's drawing or model as a pattern for a life-sized stuffed doll or an animal, stitched and sewn with an adult's help. Or make a set of costume pieces from his or her sketches and descriptions.
- Transform a closet in your child's room into an invention space designed for play and exploration. A closet, with doors removed and simple remodeling, can become a science lab, a theater stage, an art space, a rocket ship, a planetarium, and so much more!
- Have a treehouse, playhouse, climbing set, or other play structure built from designs developed by your child. Start the planning with modeling sets, blocks, or even recycled materials.
- Help your child transform a drawing or painting into a wall-sized mural. Use a grid method or a projected image to enlarge the original.
- Create a professional book-on-demand with your child's stories, art, and/or photos using Blurb, iPhoto, Lulu, or one of the other online publishers. Give copies to grandparents and other relatives as special gifts.
- Plan a family vacation or even a weekend excursion to realize a special interest, passion, or consuming curiosity for each family member in turn. This

could even be a "staycation," with special activities within your own city or within reach of a day's travel.

Going the Extra Mile with Everyday Routines

It is not enough to merely make it through a day—as parents, we must imagine how a day can be sustaining, renewing, fulfilling, and surprising. Every day should feed our minds with new ideas, stimulate our senses with its sounds and sights, and bring us moments of joy, excitement, and beauty. We must imagine what it would take every day to do this, as these kinds of experience are essential for a creative life, no matter our age. What cultivates creativity? Here are some approaches to consider:

What if:

- Before we purchased new objects for the home, we carefully considered the color, texture, and other qualities?
- If when we add something new, we let go of something no longer needed (including activities as well as stuff)?
- We have strict rules about noise and litter pollution inside and outside the home?
- We each take a turn creating a centerpiece or conversation piece for meals?
- We take routine trips to the library for picture books that make us see things differently?
- We select special music as a background for different everyday routines?
- We watch TV as if we were famous critics and discuss what we noticed, liked, and disliked?
- We share a digital toy, tool, or video at a weekly online show-and-tell session.

Quality time may be an overused phrase, but it is the most important thing a parent can provide that nurtures a child's sense of him- or herself as a worthy, contributing, valued member of the family. What special time treats can you fit into everyday routines, weekends, evenings together? Can you talk together? Or simply listen? Imagine? Collect rocks, leaves, stamps, or sounds? Experiment? Work? Play? Exercise? Build? Cook or sew? Draw or paste? Knit? Act or sing? Design? Dance? Write or read? Pretend or practice? Laugh? Photograph? Remember and share stories? Climb or run? Garden? Paint? Play drums? You don't need to be an expert. You don't need to know much more than your child does (and you may know even less once you hit on one of his or her strong suits). Do what you think your child will love using the clues you collect from your own observations and intuitions. Design your everyday context to support each child's individual creative potential.

What Next?

Now, where to go from here? Kids who are a bit older (say, age seven or more) with these understandings under their belts will be ready to exercise the more meta-cognitive thinking skills that are unfolding developmentally. They can put their strengths to work with small groups of kids who are like-minded and who work/play with more expertise or with a group beginning to collaborate. Find a local pro—it could be a coach, an artist, a business owner, or a gardener, anyone with a desire to share with the next generation—who can take their thinking to a new place. Children are interested in mastery of subjects they find meaningful.

Mix it up! Try inventing solutions for neighborhood or community-related problems with a small but diverse group of creative thinkers. Real problems are more meaningful than ones in textbooks. Parents can help out by organizing an impromptu summer camp or after-school club where children tackle an issue, topic, or problem important to them: Littering or trash-dumping, bullying at school, recycling, attitudes about body image and physical fitness. Find experts (volunteers or people hired by sharing fees with other families) to help as needed.

Ask big questions! Problems that require many kinds of ideas coming from people with different strengths will enhance analytical thinking skills. It's the beginning of systems thinking, and a great foundation for the future world of work.

Be brave! Gather your common sense, your best intuitions, your analytical skills, your long-term concern for your child's future, and . . . dive in. Design special times, resources, and approaches that support each child's unique mind and imagination. We will all thank you.

FUNdamental Tips for Parents
1. IT'S WORTH IT!
It's worth the trouble and the time and the thinking and the mess! With the pressures on parents today to provide lessons, media gadgets, and all the stuff guaranteed to help your child (and fill all his or her time), it can feel as if you're going

against the grain to protect open playtime and allow time for daydreams—even boredom. Finding a balance between structured learning and open space for imaginative play honors and extends your child's unique inventive potential and creates a priceless legacy.

2. BE A BIG MIRROR
A big part of nurturing your child's inventive potential is simply your own unspoken positive attitude and the willing support you provide to your child.

3. BACK TO THE FUTURE
Making deep and elemental connections with the real world through firsthand sensory information is one important key to building a strong, fluent, and creative mind. In our post-modern time, this often means a return to the world outside, leaving behind the electronic boxes inside our homes. Cognitive tools for this firsthand exploration—observation, collection, communication through and with sight, smell, taste, sound, movement, and touch—are the best equipment we can give kids for their future.

4. USE OPEN-ENDED STRUCTURES
Guiding a child's thinking is easier when parents whittle down the wide-open world to create viewpoints for young eyes. Provide focus (e.g., ask your child to "collect twenty different shapes of leaves," not merely to "look at trees and plants") or specific problems to solve (make a birthday card for Gram with this paper, these pens, and these stickers). We call these "open-ended structures" and have used them throughout the New World Kids program.

5. POTENT PLAYTIMES
Active, imaginative play that children initiate has been proven by cognitive researchers to be deeply important to growing minds. "Playing like" and "pretending" are thinking in action and let children rehearse for real life without the worry of consequences.

6. BE FLEXIBLE
Use your own best ideas to design activities, spaces, and materials to elicit your child's inventive thinking. This can be a messy process—it's always a bit experimental and may not produce the results you envision (and likely not what you would have done yourself). That's okay. What we do with our children as we

engage their imaginations and creative thinking is far more about the process than the product.

7. FORGET COMPETITION

This is not a race. It is the opposite. Finding a child's special gifts and mirroring them back is what makes the "aha!" happen and creates the mental space for ideas. Finding your child's gifts is a process nurtured by parental "antennae," not by competition.

8. JOIN IN

Sometimes setting the scene, planning the trip, supplying the viewpoint or the materials, and then standing back to watch what unfolds is enough. Sometimes, getting down on the floor, playing the game, or sewing the specially designed dog's costume is essential. Join the fun when asked. This is memory making.

9. KEEP IT LIGHT

Keep the emphasis on playfulness—if children feel the weight of a parent's expectation, imagination is inhibited. Putting a child in the position of trying to please is not what it's about. Enjoy the surprises. Play detective.

10. ENLIST GRANDPARENTS

Get help. Grandparents, favorite uncles, or other special adults are in a perfect position to help hold the big picture for your child. They don't have to worry about homework, soccer practice, and carpools, after all. They might have time to play and can be great advocates for young creators. Bring them into the picture with ideas, plans, outings, and events. They may even be waiting to be asked!

11. THINK DRAMA—USE SCALE

"Blowing up an idea" so that it can be seen is a good way to a underscore a child's imagination. For example, help your child make a real play and invite an audience, or cook and serve a special recipe invention to guests, or make a six-foot painting and feature it on the porch. Enlarging the scale helps kids see their ideas at work— and makes them really important and memorable.

12. USE "SCRATCH" MATERIALS

Think about how many good things to eat can be made from scratch ingredients like flour, butter, eggs, and cream! Apply those guidelines to the materials and toys you provide for your children. Many of today's toys demand a narrow range of responses from children, limiting their associative value. Recall the fun children have had for centuries with sticks, mud, rocks, sand, clay, wood scraps, and string. Make sure these kinds of scratch materials are part of your child's playtimes.

13. TEMPER EXPECTATIONS

When your child is in the midst of a grand experiment of some kind, it's easy to get carried away and want to impose your own ideas and wishes, or think what you would do is what your child should do. Keep the big picture at the forefront of your mind and remember that children don't necessarily need a finished product to grow ideas.

14. EXPAND DEFINITIONS OF "INTERACTIVE"

Many toys and games advertise "interactivity" for the child, but often that means very few choices to make or play that is quite formulaic. The biggest kind of interactive happened long before they even coined the word. It's common sense.

15. SEE KID CONCOCTIONS AS IMPORTANT INFORMATION

Closely observe the kinds of play your child comes up with on his own time—in a waiting room, when there's just a piece of paper and pen, with a buddy in the backyard, or at the park. You'll be able to compile an ever-more-accurate profile of his individual strengths. Sometimes this is easier when you can also watch other children and note the differences. It's not about "better or worse"—and it's bound to be different than your own strengths. Step back and collect this visual information as pure data to help you both refine and extend your next creative ideas for your child.

Reflections

"The world is so full of a number of things,
I'm sure we should all be as happy as kings."
—*Robert Louis Stevenson*

Reflection—looking at the internal mirror of our thoughts and actions—is an important part of the creative process for all of us—parents, children, and authors too. We see in our reflecting mind's eye a kaleidoscope of images, impressions, and data about the "metacognitive" (that layer that has to do with thinking about—witnessing—our own thinking).

Reflecting upon one's process always leads to unfolding paths—"what ifs," "what nexts"—to new entry points and new points of departure. As we reflect back over the material we've presented in this book, we hope we've made the case for the importance of the individual creative potential in children's lives today. We also hope to have given parents some basic tools and ideas for identifying and enhancing each child's special brand of creativity.

We've purposely avoided talking much about digital technology. What we want to address is the thinking behind the images and icons and sound and motion that pour out of the monitors and screens—not the screens themselves. It's kind of like saying that writing is about more than pencils.

Whether the tools you and your children use are as simple as clay and paste, or as advanced as digital cameras, CSS, and podcasting, the creative content is more than the form it takes. Heading "back to the boards" is the way the choreographer Martha Graham described her creative necessity. And that also tells us we each must begin with our own individually unique perspective in order to create with power and fluency. All the fancy tools in the world do not make a great work of art or science, architecture or astronomy, literature or lunar exploration. The idea and passion always precede the technology.

This book describes a methodology for peeling back labels, rediscovering a more elemental way of viewing the world and ourselves, one that encourages describing but not defining, contrasting but not judging, curiosity instead of right answers. We advocate engaging the primary sensory data that can spawn many ways of knowing and many forms of expression.

Honing the observation skills that build sensory awareness drives attention deep into the world around us. As many seem more and more wed to exploration via the virtual, this book is an argument for real life, real trips, hands-on real stuff. (It's the broadest bandwidth there is.)

The process of consciously making associations outside conventional boundaries can be an ongoing activity of daily life, one that is most effectively guided and modeled by parents. Putting the creative process into practice at home builds powerful thinking templates for children to follow.

Finally, to close this book, we once more step back from the day-to-day path to take the long view:

We need all the children now.

We need the ones who are hard-wired for movement—they will become the dancers, athletes, coaches—the ones who have to move to think.

We need the ones who are especially sensitive to the vibrations and needs of other people and animals—they are the potential police officers, dramatists, vets, teachers, biologists, managers, psychologists, healers—the ones who have to feel to think.

We need the ones who naturally think in 3-D—the future architects, surveyors, industrial designers, sculptors, homebuilders, urban planners, masons, engineers—the ones who need to experience space to think.

We need the ones who experience the world in images—the next photojournalists, graphic and web designers, filmmakers—the ones who think through their eyes.

We need the linear thinkers—the potential writers, storytellers, mathematicians, planners, draftsmen, logicians, playwrights, chemists—the ones who think best in linear arcs.

We need the ones who are innately attuned to the earth and her cycles—the budding botanists, cosmologists, farmers, astronomers, conservationists—the ones who naturally think in the larger patterns of our planet.

We need the ones who touch—the next weavers, chefs, physicians, carpenters, potters, gardeners, industrial designers—the ones who think with their hands.

We need the ones who innately recognize sonic power—the next composers, birders, musicians, singers, acoustic engineers—the ones who think in sound.

Please note that the careers listed come from a twentieth-century lexicon. They don't even scratch the surface of what lies just over the horizon in the immediate future. Currently, the "30,000-foot view" of our twenty-first century presents an awesome spectrum, one that spans large-scale and critical problems of global survival, to amazing discoveries and possible solutions to those problems in diverse and overlapping fields of study.

Reflecting on this near future brings our children's educational needs into a sharper focus. As we noted in the introduction to this book, our schools—even the best of them—seem stuck in a pedagogy of the past. Assurance that our children can participate successfully in this time of unparalleled change and shifting boundaries of the future will require their best individual creative thinking.

The "back to basics" clarion call is of limited reach. It neither encompasses the myriad media in young lives nor provides the thinking tools for innovation that our children need now and tomorrow. At this time, parents are the literal keys to opening the doors of change.

We want our "new world kids" to be confident of the gifts they bring into the world and confident in themselves as creators. Each of these children embodies an absolutely unique perspective, and, collectively, they need the clear vision and the sure footing to carry us all into the next Renaissance.

The future needs all the children now.

Booklist for Parents

This list of children's books highlights the different elements of the Sensory Alphabet. It is just a place to begin, by no means complete. Special thanks to Nina Carlson for her inspiration.

Line

Follow the Line by Laura Ljungkvist
Follow the Line Through the House by Laura Ljungkvist
Follow the Line Around the World by Laura Ljungkvist
Lines That Wiggle by Candace Whitman
Tommaso and the Missing Line by Matteo Pericoli
The Pencil by Allan Ahlberg

Color

One by Kathryn Otoshi
Little Blue and Little Yellow by Leo Lionni
Planting a Rainbow by Lois Ehlert
Mouse Paint by Ellen Stoll Walsh
A Color of His Own by Leo Lionni
The Colors of Us by Karen Katz
Colors by Pantone

Texture

Spiky, Slimy, Smooth: What Is Texture? by Jane Brocket
Jennie's Hat by Ezra Jack Keats
Is It Rough? Is It Smooth? Is It Shiny? by Tana Hoban
Four Fur Feet by Margaret Wise Brown
Tar Beach by Faith Ringgold
The Fabrics of Fairy Tale by Tanya Robyn Batt

Shape

Shapes, Shapes, Shapes by Tana Hoban
Shape by David Goodman
Perfect Square by Michael Hall
Shapes That Roll by Karen Berman Nagel

Color Zoo by Lois Ehlert
Mouse Shapes by Ellen Stoll Walsh

Movement
My Friends/Mis Amigos by Taro Gomi
Clap Your Hands by Lorinda Bryan Cauley
Jiggle, Wiggle, Prance by Sally Noll
Giraffes Can't Dance by Giles Andreae
Hop Jump by Ellen Stoll Walsh
From Head to Toe by Eric Carle

Sound
The Cow That Went OINK by Bernard Most
The Piggy in the Puddle by Charlotte Pomerantz
Peace at Last by Jill Murphy
Mr. Brown Can Moo! Can You? by Dr. Seuss
Click, Clack, Splish, Splash by Doreen Cronin
Polar Bear, Polar Bear, What Do You Hear? by Eric Carle

Rhythm
Press Here by Hervé Tullet
Wild Wild Sunflower Child Anna by Nancy White Carlstrom
Quick as a Cricket by Audrey Wood
Bein' With You This Way by W. Nikola-Lisa
Hand, Hand, Fingers, Thumb by Al Perkins
Doing the Animal Bop by Jan Ormerod

Space
A House Is a House for Me by Mary Ann Hoberman
The Mitten by Jan Brett
Anno's Counting Book by Mitsumasa Anno
Mr. Archimedes' Bath by Pamela Allen
Zero by Kathyrn Otoshi
Bear's Bargain by Frank Asch
The Best Nest by P.D. Eastman

Light
Shadow by Suzy Lee
Moondance by Frank Asch
Moonbear's Shadow by Frank Asch
Papa, Please Get the Moon for Me by Eric Carle
The Very Lonely Firefly by Eric Carle
Shadows and Reflections by Tana Hoban

Other Books
An Egg Is Quiet by Dianna Hutts Aston (shape, color)
Alphabeasties: And Other Amazing Types by Sharon Werner (shape, line, texture)
The Graphic Alphabet by David Pelletier (shape, line)
Bruno Munari's Zoo by Bruno Munari (shape, line, texture)
Swirl by Swirl: Spirals in Nature by Joyce Sidman and Beth Krommes (line, texture, shape)
A Butterfly Is Patient by Dianna Hutts Aston (color, texture)
Beautiful Oops! by Barney Saltzberg (color, shape, line, texture)
In My World by Lois Ehlert (shape, color, movement, sound)

Bibliography

Anderson, L.W., D. R. Krathwohl, Peter W. Airasian, Kathleen A. Cruikshank, Richard E. Mayer, Paul R. Pintrich, James Raths, and Merlin C. Wittrock, eds. 2000. *A Taxonomy for Learning, Teaching, and Assessing: A Revision of Bloom's Taxonomy of Educational Objectives.* Upper Saddle River, NJ: Allyn and Bacon.

Armstrong, Thomas. 2009. *Multiple Intelligences in the Classroom,* 3rd ed. Alexandria, VA: Association for Supervision and Curriculum Development.

Bransford, John D., Ann Brown, and Rodney Cocking, eds. 2000. *How People Learn: Brain, Mind, Experience, and School.* Washington, D.C.: National Academy Press.

Brazelton, T. Berry. 1983. *Infants and Mothers,* revised edition. New York: Dell.

Bridgeland, John M., John J. DiIulio Jr., Karen Burke Morison. 2006. *The Silent Epidemic: Perspectives From High School Dropouts.* Prepared by Civic Enterprises in association with Peter D. Hart Research Associates for the Bill and Melinda Gates Foundation.

Bruner, J. S., A. Jolly, & K. Sylva, eds. 1976. *Play: Its Role in Evolution and Development.* New York: Basic Books.

Bruner, Jerome. 1966. *Toward a Theory of Instruction.* Cambridge, MA: Belknap Press of Harvard University Press.

Caine, R.N. and Geoffrey Caine. 1994. *Making Connections: Teaching and the Human Brain.* Upper Saddle River, NJ: Dale Seymour Publications.

Caine, R.N. and Geoffrey Caine. 1997. *Education on the Edge of Possibility.* Alexandria, VA: Association for Supervision and Curriculum Development.

Carr, Austin. 2010. "The Most Important Leadership Quality for CEOs? Creativity." *Fast Company,* May 18. www.fastcompany.com/1648943/creativity_the_most_impotant_leadership_quality_for_ceos_study.

Csikszentmihalyi, Mihaly. 1990. *Creativity: The Work and Lives of 91 Eminent People.* New York: HarperCollins.

Edwards, C., L. Gandini, and G. Forman, eds. 1998. *The Hundred Languages of Children: The Reggio Emilia Approach—Advanced Reflections.* Westport, CT: Ablex.

Elffers, Joost. 1997. *Play With Your Food.* New York: MetroBooks.

Gardner, Howard. 1999. *The Disciplined Mind.* New York: Simon and Shuster.

Herbert, Cynthia Ridgeway. 1982. *Early Forms of Metacognition in the Imaginative*

Play of Young Children. Doctoral Dissertation. Houston, TX: University of Houston.

Herbert, Cynthia. 2009. *New World Kids at School: The Teacher's Guide to Creative Thinking.* Austin, TX: Foundry Media.

Jensen, Eric. 1999. *Teaching With the Brain in Mind.* Alexandria, VA: Association for Supervision and Curriculum Development.

Jensen, Eric. 2001. *Arts With the Brain in Mind.* Alexandria, VA: Association for Supervision and Curriculum Development.

McGonigal, Jane. 2010. *Reality is Broken: Why Games Make Us Better and How They Can Change the World.* New York: Penguin Press.

McLuhan, Marshall. 1964. *Understanding Media: The Extensions of Man.* New York: McGraw Hill.

McLuhan, Marshall, with Quentin Fiore. 1967. *The Medium Is the Massage.* New York: Bantam Books.

Montessori, Maria. 2011. *The Montessori Method.* CreateSpace.

Neisser, Ulric and Ira Hyman. 1999. *Memory Observed: Remembering in Natural Contexts,* 2nd ed. New York: Worth Publishers.

Piaget, Jean. 1974. *To Understand Is to Invent.* New York: Penguin.

Pink, Daniel. 2006. *A Whole New Mind: Why Right-Brainers Will Rule the Future.* New York: Riverhead Books.

Robinson, Ken. 2011. *Out of Our Minds: Leaning to Be Creative.* West Sussex: Capstone Publishing Limited.

Sousa, David A. 2005. *How the Brain Learns,* 3rd ed. Thousand Oaks, CA: Corwin Press.

Tomlinson, Carol Ann. 1999. *Differentiated Instruction: Responding to the Needs of All Learners.* Alexandria, VA: Association for Supervision and Curriculum Development.

Vygotsky, L.S. 1978. *Mind in Society: The Development of Higher Psychological Processes.* Cambridge: Harvard University Press.

Whyte, David. 2001. *Crossing the Unknown Sea: Work as a Pilgrimage of Identity.* New York: Riverhead Books.

Acknowledgments

We gratefully acknowledge the contributions made to this book and its philosophy from all the teachers, children, and parents along the way throughout nearly a half century of creative exploration and experimentation.

We are deeply indebted to all who were, long ago, part of Kitty Baker and Jearnine Wagner's Baylor Children's Theatre, the "mother ship" that gave birth to the Dallas Children's Theatre, the Unlimited Potential program, and eventually, the Learning About Learning Educational Foundation.

Learning About Learning was the crucible for our research in creativity, our lab school, and our work in the San Antonio community—and holds a special place in our hearts. We acknowledge the extraordinary gifts and work of our colleagues Julia Jarrell and Nancy Busch and also wish to thank the others who were integral to its influence as a national model and research institute for arts in education.

Lately, these ideas found programmatic form at the Aldrich Contemporary Museum in Ridgefield, Connecticut, and we appreciate the far-sighted vision of Director Harry Philbrick and Education Director Nina Carlson for extending the idea of what museum education can be. Big Thought's President, Gigi Antoni, and Director of Programs, Margie Reese, have reached out and helped us bring New World Kids programs into after-school settings for Dallas children. These collaborators and others have pushed the boundaries of creative learning opportunities for kids, and we thank them. The images of children from these programs enrich our words here.

It was Liener Temerlin and Stan Richards, the celebrated admen from Dallas, who first said, "It's time for this." Their encouragement has inspired and enlivened this effort—and we extend our appreciation.

Many thanks to our partners at Greenleaf Book Group and to our editors Amy McIlwaine, who brought a young mom's eye to the work, and especially to Tina Posner, for her special expertise and experience in helping to shape the content.

And, our dearest thank you is for our partners, Richard Marcus, Linda Cuéllar, and Jaime G. Garcia—for their patience, support, encouragement, and the many close and helpful readings during the time it took to produce this book.

About the Authors

Susan Marcus, Susie Monday, and Cynthia Herbert, PhD, are deeply experienced researchers, program designers, educators, trainers, and authors. They were co-founders of the Learning About Learning Educational Foundation, a future-oriented organization in San Antonio, Texas (1971–1985).

Cynthia, a developmental psychologist, led LAL's Lab School, recognized as a national model for learning through the arts. She is also the former Director of the Texas Alliance for Education and the Arts and a specialist in Differentiated Education, providing educators with strategies and support to help diverse children learn, create, and thrive.

Susie has also worked as a journalist, children's museum designer, and educational consultant. She maintains a Texas Hill Country studio as a textile artist and is an adjunct faculty member of the Southwest School of Art in San Antonio.

Susan has also worked as a consultant to museums and as a children's program designer. She is the coauthor, with Cynthia, of *Everychild's Everyday* (Doubleday) and *When I Was Just Your Age* (University of North Texas Press), and, with Susie, *New World Kids* (FoundryMedia).

Responding to the educational imperatives of the 21st century, they have once again collaborated, forming The Foundry in Austin to produce programs in creative thinking for children and parents, and professional development for educators.

Photo Credits

Page	Position	Credit
cover		Dimitris66/iStock
35	1	Susie Monday
36	1	Allison V Smith
	2	Allison V Smith
37	1	Allison V Smith
	2	Susan Marcus
38	1	Susan Marcus
	2	Allison V Smith
39	1	Susan Marcus
	2	Allison V Smith
55	1	Susan Marcus
59	1	Susan Marcus
60	1	Susan Marcus
	2	Susan Marcus
	3	Susan Marcus
	4	Susan Marcus
61	1	Shutterstock
	2	Shutterstock
	3	Shutterstock
75	1–9	Allison V Smith
77	1	Susan Marcus
	2	Susan Marcus
	3	Susan Marcus
	4	Shutterstock
78	1	Susan Marcus
	2	Shutterstock
	3	Shutterstock
	4	Susan Marcus
	5	Shutterstock
	6	Susan Marcus
	7	Shutterstock
79	1	Susan Marcus
	2	Shutterstock
	3	Susan Marcus
	4	Susan Marcus
	5	Shutterstock
	6	Shutterstock
	7	Shutterstock
81	1	Shutterstock
	2	Allison V Smith
	3	Allison V Smith
	4	Shutterstock
	5	Shutterstock
	6	KarSol/ Shutterstock.com
	7	Shutterstock
	8	Allison V Smith
83	1	Shutterstock
	2	Susan Marcus
	3	Susan Marcus
	4	Shutterstock

Page	Position	Credit
84	1	Shutterstock
	2	Shutterstock
	3	Shutterstock
84	4	Shutterstock
	5	Thomas Barrat/ Shutterstock.com
	6	Shutterstock
	7	Susie Monday
85	1	Susie Monday
	2	Susan Marcus
	3	Susan Marcus
	4	Susan Marcus
	5	Susan Marcus
	6	Susan Marcus
	7	Shutterstock
	8	Susan Marcus
87	1	Susan Marcus
	2	Susan Marcus
	3	Shutterstock
	4	Shutterstock
	5	Susan Marcus
	6	Allison V Smith
	7	Shutterstock
	8	Shutterstock
	9	Allison V Smith
89	1	Susan Marcus
	2	Susan Marcus
	3	Allison V Smith
	4	Susan Marcus
90	1	Susan Marcus
	2	Allison V Smith
	3	Allison V Smith
	4	Allison V Smith
	5	Shutterstock
	6	Susan Marcus
	7	Shutterstock
91	1	Susan Marcus
	2	Shutterstock
	3	Shutterstock
	4	Shutterstock
	5	Susan Marcus
	6	Susan Marcus
	7	Susan Marcus
93	1	B Stefanov / Shutterstock.com
	2	Shutterstock
	3	Susan Marcus
	4	Susan Marcus
	5	Shutterstock
	6	Shutterstock
	7	Allison V Smith
	8	Allison V Smith
	9	Shutterstock
	10	Allison V Smith

Page	Position	Credit
95	1	Allison V Smith
95	2	Allison V Smith
	3	Allison V Smith
	4	Allison V Smith
96	1	Shutterstock
	2	Allison V Smith
	3	iStock
	4	Susan Marcus
	5	Dr_Flash/ Shutterstock.com
	6	Tony Sanchez Poy /Shutterstock.com
	7	Susan Marcus
97	1	Susan Marcus
	2	Susan Marcus
	3	Shutterstock
	4	Susie Monday
	5	Allison V Smith
	6	Susan Marcus
	7	Susan Marcus
99	1	Allison V Smith
	2	Susan Marcus
	3	Susan Marcus
	4	Vladimir Korostyshevskiy / Shutterstock.com
	5	Shutterstock
	6	Shutterstock
	7	Shutterstock
	8	Shutterstock
	9	Allison V Smith
	10	Allison V Smith
102	1	Shutterstock
	2	Shutterstock
	3	Susan Marcus
	4	Shutterstock
	5	Allison V Smith
	6	Susan Marcus
	7	Shutterstock
103	1	Shutterstock
	2	Susan Marcus
	3	Susan Marcus
	4	Shutterstock
	5	Susan Marcus
	6	Susan Marcus
	7	Susan Marcus
105	1	Susie Monday
	2	Allison V Smith
	3	iStock
	4	Cynthia Herbert
	5	Allison V Smith
	6	Heather LaVelle / Shutterstock.com
	7	Allison V Smith

Page	Position	Credit
107	1	Allison V Smith
107	2	Susie Monday
108	1	Allison V Smith
	2	Shutterstock
	3	iStock
	4	Allison V Smith
	5	Shutterstock
	6	Susan Marcus
109	1	Vladimir Korostyshevskiy/ Shutterstock.com
	2	Susie Monday
	3	Susan Marcus
	4	Susan Marcus
	5	Shutterstock
	6	Susie Monday
111	1	Allison V Smith
	2	Allison V Smith
	3	egd/ Shutterstock.com
	4	Allison V Smith
	5	Susan Marcus
	6	Allison V Smith
	7	Allison V Smith
	8	Allison V Smith
	9	Allison V Smith
114	1	Susan Marcus
	2	Susan Marcus
	3	Susan Marcus
	4	iStock
	5	Allison V Smith
	6	Susan Marcus
	7	Susan Marcus
115	1	Susan Marcus
	2	Shutterstock
	3	Shutterstock
	4	Shutterstock
	5	Susan Marcus
	6	Susan Marcus
119	1	Allison V Smith
	2	Allison V Smith
	3	Susan Marcus
	4	Shutterstock
	5	Allison V Smith
	6	Studio38/ Shutterstock.com
	7	Allison V Smith
	8	Allison V Smith
	9	Shutterstock
121	1	Allison V Smith
	2	Allison V Smith
	3	Allison V Smith
	4	Susan Marcus
	5	Susan Marcus

Page	Position	Credit
122	1	Susan Marcus
122	2	Susan Marcus
	3	iStock
	4	Susan Marcus
	5	Shutterstock
	6	Susan Marcus
	7	Susie Monday
123	1	Shutterstock
	2	KUCO/ Shutterstock.com
	3	Shutterstock
	4	Shutterstock
	5	Nina Carlson
	6	Susan Marcus
	7	Shutterstock
127	1	Shutterstock
	2	Shutterstock
	3	Susan Marcus
	4	Shutterstock
	5	Allison V Smith
	6	Allison V Smith
	7	Allison V Smith
	8	Allison V Smith
	9	Shutterstock
129	1	Allison V Smith
	2	Allison V Smith
	3	Allison V Smith
	4	Shutterstock
130	1	Allison V Smith
	2	Allison V Smith
	3	Shutterstock
	4	Shutterstock
	5	Shutterstock
	6	Susan Marcus
	7	Allison V Smith
	8	Susan Marcus
131	1	Allison V Smith
	2	Shutterstock
	3	Shutterstock
	4	Susan Marcus
	5	Susan Marcus
	6	Shutterstock
131	7	Allison V Smith
136–144	all	Susan Marcus